PSYCHOANALYSIS OF DEVELOPMENTAL ARRESTS

Theory and Treatment

PSYCHOANALYSIS OF DEVELOPMENTAL ARRESTS

Theory and Treatment

ROBERT D. STOLOROW

AND

FRANK M. LACHMANN

INTERNATIONAL UNIVERSITIES PRESS, INC.

New York

616.8582
S 875

Copyright © 1980, International Universities Press

All rights reserved. No part of this book may be reproduced by any means, nor translated into a machine language, without the written permission of the publisher.

Third Printing, 1983

Library of Congress Cataloging in Publication Data

Stolorow, Robert D
  Psychoanalysis of developmental arrests.

  Bibliography: p.
  Includes index.
  1. Psychoanalysis. 2. Personality, Disorders
of. I. Lachmann, Frank M., joint author.
II. Title.
RC506.S74   616.8'582   79-53593
ISBN 0-8236-5146-0

Manufactured in the United States of America

To Annette Lachmann and Virginia Stolorow

Contents

Acknowledgments

Among the many people to whom we are indebted, several deserve special mention. One of us (F.L.) would like to acknowledge the influence of the teachings of Martin Bergmann. For both of us, the innovative, seminal writings of Heinz Kohut have provided a unique frame of reference from which to study new terrain. We are especially grateful to our wives, Annette Lachmann and Virginia Stolorow, whose tolerance and empathic understanding enabled our ideas to develop from their early prestages to their present form.

A substantial part of our book consists of modified versions of papers that have appeared in various psychoanalytic journals. We express our thanks to the editors and publishers of these journals for granting us permission to include this material. Chapters 2, 3, 7, and part of 8 appeared in the *International Journal of Psycho-Analysis,* volumes 56, 58, 60; chapters 4, 5, and 6 appeared in the *Psychoanalytic Quarterly,* volumes 44, 45, 47; part of chapter 7 appeared in the *American Journal of Psychoanalysis,* volume 34/4, pp. 351-353.

Finally, we wish to thank Natalie Altman, whose skillful editing helped us integrate these papers, along with new material, into a coherent book.

1

Introduction

Freud's (1933) dictum, "Where id was, there ego shall be," though intended as a goal for psychoanalytic treatment, has turned out as well to describe the direction in which psychoanalytic theory has evolved. Id psychology and the study of psychosexual development has been supplemented by ego psychology and the exploration of the development of self and object representations. Where once the primary developing unit was the instinctual drive, now "autonomous" ego functions (Hartmann, 1939), and, more recently, separation and individuation (Mahler et al., 1975), the maturation of self-object-affect units (Kernberg, 1976), the evolution of the representational world (Sandler and Rosenblatt, 1962; Stolorow and Atwood, 1979), the transformation of archaic selfobject[1] configurations (Kohut, 1971), and other developmental concepts have been proposed.

Freud conceived of psychoanalysis as a theory, a research tool, and a method of treatment. Expansion in each of these areas has influenced the others and has widened the *clinical* scope of psychoanalysis.

---

[1] We use the term *selfobject* to refer to the concept of an archaic object which is experienced as incompletely distinguished from the self and/or which serves to restore or maintain the sense of self (Kohut, 1971, 1977).

1

With regard to the expansion of psychoanalytic theory, the writings of Hartmann (1939) have been especially relevant for our work. His postulations concerning the conflict-free sphere of ego functioning as well as his contributions to the genetic and adaptive points of view have aided analysts in their study of severe pathology and developmental deficits (see Blanck and Blanck, 1974). Through Hartmann and those influenced by him (e.g., Jacobson, 1964), psychoanalysis has moved toward embracing a model rooted in human developmental concepts.

Research in child development, especially the work of Spitz (1965) and Mahler et al. (1975), has offered both observations and constructs which have supplemented genetic reconstructions of the early preverbal period. The influence of these authors will be apparent throughout this book.

The contrasting clinical contributions of Kohut (1971, 1977) and Kernberg (1975, 1976) have provided analysts with the crucial questions to raise. Viewed from a historical perspective, the contributions of Kernberg can be seen as an attempt to combine Freudian ego psychology with the object relations concepts of Melanie Klein. Like Klein, Kernberg has emphasized the role of pregenital aggression and primitive defenses against it in the genesis of narcissistic and borderline psychopathology. Kohut, on the other hand, offers an innovative clinical approach to these disorders, centering on the developmental transformation of archaic states.

We do not believe that patients diagnosed today as having narcissistic and borderline disorders are a new species produced by modern society. The difficulties encountered in the treatment of these patients have been reported by generations of analysts, from Freud (1914a) and Abraham (1919) onward. We do believe that the theoretical, observational, and clinical advances described above have contributed to the increasing interest or decreasing reluctance with which analysts have approached these patients. Psychoanalysis as a theory that has guided the treatment of the psychoneuroses has been extended to encompass more than psychopathology rooted in intrapsychic conflict. Severe characterological, narcissistic, borderline, and psychotic disorders are now treatable within the framework of the more encompassing theory. Revisions, refinements, and elaborations of psychoanalytic developmental psychology have placed the analyst in a better position to understand these "difficult-to-treat" patients. Efforts to understand and treat these more severe forms of psychopathology have highlighted the central importance of the lines of development that lead to the structuralization of the "representational world" (Sandler and Rosenblatt, 1962; Stolorow and Atwood, 1979)—that is, to the establishment and consolidation of a subjective world of differentiated and integrated self and object representations.

In the earliest phase of infancy, self and object representations are undifferentiated. Gradually the neonate acquires the capacity to discriminate between his own sensations and the objects from which they are derived (Jacobson, 1964). Thus, perhaps the first developmental task to face the infant, central to the beginning articulation and structuralization of his representational world, is the differentiation or subjective separation of self representations from representations of his primary objects, principally the mother, and the rudimentary establishment of self-object boundaries (Mahler et al., 1975). An example of an early infantile experience of partial self-object confusion would be the toddler who believes his mother knows his thoughts or has put thoughts into his head. The small child's incomplete attainment of self-object boundaries makes it both necessary and possible for him to rely upon parental figures as "selfobjects" whose idealized attributes and mirror functions provide him with the self-cohesion and self-continuity that he cannot yet maintain on his own (Kohut, 1971).

A second characteristic of the very young infant's experience is his inability to integrate or synthesize representations with contrasting affective colorations. Thus, a second developmental task, coincident with that of self-object differentiation, is the synthesis of object representations colored with positive affects (e.g., images of an "all-good" mother) and object representations colored with negative affects (e.g., images of an "all-bad" mother) into an integrated representation of a whole object with both positive and negative qualities, coupled with a similar synthesis of affectively contrasting self representations into an integrated representation of the whole self (Kernberg, 1976).

From the standpoint of the object world, the consolidation of differentiated and integrated representations is reflected in the achievement of "object constancy"—the capacity to sustain and relate to an enduring image of another person who is valued for his real (positive and negative) qualities and is recognized as a separate individual with needs and feelings of his own (Burgner and Edgcumbe, 1972). From the standpoint of the self, the consolidation of differentiated and integrated representations is reflected in the establishment of a cohesive image of the self which is temporally stable and has an affective coloration more or less independent of immediate environmental supports. Such "self constancy" has been described in terms of the subjective sense of identity (Erikson, 1956) and the continuity of self-esteem (Jacobson, 1964; Kohut, 1971).

Failures to attain adequate self and object constancy have been attributed largely to deficiencies in early care as a consequence of psychopathology in the parents. Examples of such deficiencies would be an absence of empathic responsiveness to the child's developmental requirements, extreme inconsistencies in behavior toward the child, and frequent exposure of the child to affectively unbearable sexual and aggressive scenes. When traumata such as these interfere with the structuralization of the representational world, the individual remains arrested at, or vulnerable to regressive revivals of, archaic, more or less undifferentiated and unintegrated selfobject configurations.[2] Our principal aims in this book are to elucidate the contribution of such developmental interferences and arrests to a variety of pathological states, and to spell out the implications of this understanding for the specific framing of analytic interventions and for conceptualizing the psychoanalytic situation and the course and therapeutic action of psychoanalytic therapy.

In Part I we concentrate on interferences with the consolidation of the self representation in relation to narcissistic disorders and masochistic pathology. In Part II the concept of defense is reexamined within a developmental framework. The crucial distinction between psychopathology which is the product of defenses against intrapsychic conflict and psychopathology which is the remnant of a developmental arrest at prestages of defense will be explicated. In Part III this understanding is used to shed new light on a number of clinical problems heretofore seen primarily from the standpoint of intrapsychic conflicts.

[2] Throughout this book, when we use the term *arrest* we do not mean to imply that development was completely stopped. Rather, we mean that the structuralization of the subjective world has been incomplete, uneven, or partially aborted so that the more advanced representational structures remain vulnerable to regressive dissolution.

Part I

NARCISSISM AND SELF REPRESENTATION

2

A Functional Definition
of Narcissism

The evolution of psychoanalysis has required the redefinition of many terms. As the pre-eminence of the topographic theory gave way to structural formulations, to ego psychology, and then to an emphasis on the development of self and object representations, old terms had to be adapted to new surroundings. The extension of psychoanalytically informed treatment to what were once called "narcissistic neuroses" (Freud, 1914a) has demanded a clarification of concepts, which, in the past, could remain enshrined in the untouched realms of metapsychology.

Traditional usage within the economic model and psychoanalytic drive theory defines narcissism as pertaining to the libidinal cathexis of the self. Pulver (1970) has cogently reviewed the difficulties inherent in this economic concept of narcissism. Citing the work of Apfelbaum (1965) and Holt (see Dahl, 1968), Pulver notes that the economic model and drive theory in general have been subjected to serious criticisms. Further, he argues convincingly that the nonspecific nature of the terms *li-*

bido and *self* has introduced conceptual confusion into our thinking about narcissism, so much so that the drive concept of narcissism is of little clinical use. Pulver concludes that a "serious result of this vagueness is that the concept [narcissism] has not received the elaboration in terms of ego psychology which . . . it richly deserves." This chapter is in the spirit of such an elaboration.

Since the advent of the structural theory, a trend in psychoanalytic thought has been to move away from a preoccupation with purely economic explanations toward functional explanations. Contemporary analysts are less interested in explaining mental activity primarily in terms of a hypothetical flow of psychic energies—a highly abstract level of theorizing far removed from empirical and phenomenological verification—and are more interested in understanding the multiple purposes which a given mental activity serves in the interplay of id, ego, and superego functions within the personality—a level of theorizing much closer to actual clinical observations (Waelder, 1936; Arlow and Brenner, 1964). In keeping with this trend, the following functional definition of narcissism is offered, which captures the state of our knowledge about the unique function served by those mental activities clinicians have seen as narcissistic:

Mental activity is narcissistic to the degree that its function is to maintain the structural cohesion, temporal stability, and positive affective coloring of the self representation.

In what follows, the work of those who have made significant contributions to our understanding of narcissism in functional terms is reviewed. An attempt is then made to demonstrate that a functional conception of narcissism can clarify the ambiguities and contradictions that have arisen as a result of the traditional drive concept of narcissism.

CONTRIBUTIONS TO A FUNCTIONAL
UNDERSTANDING OF NARCISSISM

Numerous authors (e.g., Arlow and Brenner, 1964; Freeman, 1964; Eisnitz, 1969) have pointed out that narcissistic activity may function as a defense, in order to ward off a multitude of object-related intrapsychic (incestuous, sadomasochistic) conflicts. An example of this orientation is Kernberg's (1975) detailed interpretation of the "splendid isolation" and cold, contemptuous attitudes of the narcissistic personality as representing a defensive retreat from dreaded object relationships characterized by intense dependency, oral envy, and primitive oral sadism, and the resulting guilt and fears of retaliation. The correctness of such interpretations in some cases cannot be doubted. However, since virtually any mental activity can serve to defend against intrapsychic conflicts and dreaded object relationships, such interpretations do not enhance our understanding of the *unique* function of activity clinicians have termed narcissistic. Hence, the brief review that follows will be restricted to explanations which have contributed to our insight into the specific and unique function of narcissistic activity as in our proposed definition.

Groundwork for a functional understanding of narcissism was provided by Hartmann's (1950) conceptual distinction between ego (a system of mental functions), self (the whole person of an individual, including his body and body parts as well as his psychic organization and its parts), and self representation (unconscious, preconscious, and conscious representations of the bodily and mental self). Taking off from Hartmann's distinction, Jacobson (1964) pointed out that narcissism is not identical with the libidinal endowment of the ego system or of ego functions, as Freud (1914a) had originally postulated. Narcissism, according to Jacobson, refers to the libidinal cathexis of the self representation, which is constituted in the course of development. While Jacobson's formulation remains rooted within the economic model, it is nevertheless very useful in delineating the arena in which narcissistic activity exercises its function—namely, the arena of the self representation.

That Freud himself was aware of the functional relationship between narcissistic activity and the maintenance of the self representation is suggested by his remark (1914a, p. 98) that "the self-regard has a very intimate connection with the narcissistic libido." Freud noted that in narcissistic object-choice the aim is to be loved and, further, that to be loved raises the self-regard. The clear implication is that the function of narcissistic object-choice is to regulate self-esteem (i.e., to maintain the positive affective coloring of the self representation). However, Freud did not carry this implication further.

It was Annie Reich who first spelled out with crystal clarity how certain patterns traditionally termed narcissistic function to maintain the self representation. In the earlier of two important papers (1953), she described how certain women may form a narcissistic object tie to an aggrandized phallic ideal in order to undo the trauma of their imagined castration and resulting sense of defect and inferiority. Union with a phallic ideal was understood as a magic method of repairing the damaged self representation and restoring injured self-esteem. In her later paper (1960), Reich suggested that various other narcissistic patterns (e.g., grandiose self-inflation, preoccupation with the body and its appearance, and ceaseless cravings for admiring attention) may represent attempts to repair damage done to the self representation by early traumatic experiences. Reich clearly interpreted clinically observed "narcissistic disturbances" as abortive attempts to restore and stabilize self-esteem.

Numerous authors have buttressed and amplified Reich's ground-breaking formulations. Elkisch (1957) observed that certain of her patients gazed at their images in the mirror in order to restore a lost sense of self-identity. Referring to the myth of Narcissus, Lichtenstein (1964, p. 52) suggested that narcissism refers not to the love of one's self but to the love of one's mirror image, and argued that "the mirror and the act of mirroring introduce problems of the emergence of a primary identity, of identity confusion, of loss of identity and of identity maintenance as well." Narcissistic object relations are to be understood as regressive efforts at maintaining identity through mirroring in the object. Eisnitz (1969) believed that narcissistic object-choices serve to stabilize and supplement a weakened self representation. Arlow and Brenner (1964), Murray (1964), Oremland and Windholz (1971), and Kernberg (1975) all noted that grandiose fantasies of magical omnipotence and unlimited entitlement may be attempts to repair various injuries to and degradations of the self representation and to avert the threat of its dissolution.

Perhaps the most detailed account of how narcissistic patterns function to maintain the self representation has been presented by Kohut (1971, 1977). The nuclear pathology in narcissistic disturbances, according to Kohut, is an absence of or defect in psychological structure that maintains self-cohesion and self-esteem. In narcissistic object relations, the object functions as a "selfobject"—that is, as a substitute for the missing or defective self-esteem-regulating psychic structure. The selfobject performs basic functions in the realm of self-esteem regulation that the individual's own psyche is unable to provide. Archaic narcissistic configurations, in which, for example, the individual requires continuous mirroring of his grandiose fantasies or merger with an aggrandized omnipotent object, are mobilized in order to solidify a fragile and precarious sense of self-cohesion and self-esteem and to avert the ultimate threat of fragmentation and structural disintegration of the self representation.

It is surprising that, despite *clinical* formulations which stress the structure-maintaining function of narcissistic activity, authors have been reluctant to take the ultimate *metapsychological* step of freeing the concept of narcissism from an economic definition it has outgrown, and of redefining narcissism in functional terms. For instance, Kohut, in his earlier work (1971), when attempting to define a narcissistic object relationship metapsychologically, says, *"Narcissism . . . is defined not by the target of the instinctual investment (i.e. whether it is the subject himself or other people) but by the nature or quality of the instinctual charge.* The small child invests other people with narcissistic cathexes and thus experiences them narcissistically . . . " (1971, p. 26). In a narcissistic object relation, the object is invested with narcissistic cathexes. But what is a narcissistic cathexis? In attempting to reconcile his seminal clinical observations with an outmoded economic concept of narcissism, Kohut presents us here with either a tautology or a speculative metapsychological proposition that there is a qualitative difference between narcissistic energies and object-related energies.[1] A way out of this conceptual mulberry bush, one that would be entirely consistent with Kohut's clinical formulations, would be to define a narcissistic object relation as one whose *function* is to maintain the cohesion, stability, and positive affective

[1] These criticisms in no way apply to Kohut's later work (1977), in which he in large part dispenses with these economic formulations and conceptualizes his discoveries in terms of a developmental phenomenology of the self. This latter framework, implicit in his earlier work, seems to us to be entirely compatible with the functional conception of narcissism presented here.

coloring of the self representation. In what follows, it will be seen that other conceptual difficulties can be cleared up by replacing the drive concept of narcissism with a functional definition.

CLARIFICATIONS ACHIEVED WITH A FUNCTIONAL DEFINITION

After a review of the literature, Pulver (1970) concluded that the term narcissism has been used clinically to refer to (1) a sexual perversion, (2) a mode of relating to objects, (3) a developmental stage, and (4) self-esteem. We shall now demonstrate that a functional definition lends clarification to our understanding of narcissism in each of these four usages. Furthermore, we shall show that a functional definition clarifies the use of narcissism as a diagnostic term, illuminates the issue of healthy versus unhealthy narcissism, and helps us to avoid certain countertransference pitfalls with narcissistic patients.

1. Narcissism as a Sexual Perversion

Narcissism as a sexual perversion refers to the taking of one's own body, or more specifically the mirror image of one's own body, as a sexual object. In current clinical thinking it is insufficient to interpret a sexual perversion solely in drive-theory terms as a psychosexual fixation (in this case, a fixation on the self as sexual object). It is also necessary to understand the functions served by perverse activity within the personality. With regard to the narcissistic perversion, Elkisch (1957) and Lichtenstein (1964) have noted that patients become preoccupied with their mirror image in order to restore and stabilize a crumbling self representation. Reich (1960), Kohut (1971, 1977), and Goldberg (1975) have observed that a

wide variety of sexual perversions may function as sexualized attempts to counteract feelings of self-depletion
and self-fragmentation, to revive the sense of having a
cohesive self, and to restore self-esteem. Hence it would
seem that a functional conception of narcissism in terms
of the maintenance of the self representation contributes
significantly to our understanding of the narcissistic
perversion and perverse activity in general. In chapter
8 we will consider this issue in greater detail, with il-
lustrative clinical material.

2. *Narcissism as a Mode of Relating to Objects*

Again following Pulver, narcissism has been used to refer
to (a) a mode of relating to the environment characterized
by a relative lack of object relations—that is, withdrawal
from overt observable relations with objects in the environment—and (b) a type of object-choice in which the
self plays a more important part than the real aspects of
the object.

   With regard to (a), Pulver points out that the difficulty
in applying the drive concept of narcissism to overt withdrawal from objects is that lack of overt object relations
does not mean that objects are not psychically
present—that is, despite defensive overt withdrawal, objects may remain intensely important intrapsychically.
Kohut (1971), too, stresses that a person's seeming isolation may cloak a wealth of object involvements. The
difficulty is cleared up by applying the functional definition of narcissism: Withdrawal behavior is narcissistic
depending on its function, or the function of the accompanying fantasies. If the withdrawal behavior and/or the
fantasies buttress the cohesion, stability, and positive
affective coloring of a threatened self representation,
then the withdrawal may be called narcissistic. This may

be contrasted with a defensive withdrawal which wards off conflicts evoked by sexual or aggressive wishes toward objects.

With regard to (b), Pulver notes, as have many others (Reich, 1953; Lichtenstein, 1964; Eisnitz, 1969; Kohut, 1971), that narcissistic object-ties may be characterized by a very intense overt attachment to external objects. In other words, increased interest in the self is not necessarily accompanied by a decreased involvement with others, as is implied in the drive concept of narcissism. Freud's (1914a) economic hypothesis that narcissism and object relationship are mutually exclusive does not appear to hold up clinically. As mentioned earlier, the contradictions spawned by the drive concept of narcissism are rather easily cleared up by a functional definition, according to which a narcissistic object-choice is defined as one whose function is to maintain the cohesiveness, stability, and positive affective coloring of the self representation. It is clear that an intensely experienced object relation can serve a primarily narcissistic function. The supposed antithesis between narcissism and object relationship is an artifact of an outmoded economic concept of narcissism.

3. Narcissism as a Developmental Stage

Though Freud's conception of narcissism as a developmental stage frequently changed (Kanzer, 1964), in his later writings (1940, p. 150) he reaffirmed his earlier theory of a stage of primary narcissism. According to this theory (Freud, 1914a), primary narcissism refers to the earliest stage in the infant's energic economy, in which all of the libido is invested in the self and object cathexes have not yet developed. Pulver's review indicates that in current usage narcissism as a developmental stage is

synonymous with primary narcissism. Pulver aptly crit-
icizes this usage on the ground that the drive concept of
primary narcissism as the libidinal cathexis of the self
does not do justice to the developmental complexities,
including the vicissitudes of object relations, which occur
during the first six to eight months of life.

Perhaps the most pointed critique of the theory of
primary narcissism can be found in the writings of Balint
(1960), who argues that most of the observations on which
Freud and others based the hypothesis of primary narcissism prove only the existence of secondary narcissism,
which occurs after frustration by the environment. Balint
suggests further that in deeply regressive states, such as
those found in psychosis and in dreamless sleep (see
Lewin, 1954), the fixation point is not primary narcissism, but rather a primitive form of relationship to a
probably undifferentiated environment. In opposition to
the theory of primary narcissism, he proposes that the
neonate is born into a primary state of intense relatedness to his environment, a state of harmonious merger
with the environment which Balint calls primary love.
According to Balint, all narcissism is secondary to this
primary love and is caused by a disturbance between the
infant and environment. Others (e.g., Rosenfeld, 1964b)
have similarly claimed that the earliest period of infancy
is characterized not by a primary state of self-absorption
but rather by primitive object relations.

The controversy over primary narcissism versus primary object relatedness appears to be another red herring
created by the drive concept of narcissism. In the earliest
infantile stage the self and object world are undifferentiated—the neonate cannot discriminate between his own
sensations and the objects from which they are derived
(Jacobson, 1964). Since self and object images are not yet
differentiated, it makes no sense to think of this earliest

neonatal stage in terms of either primary self-love or primary object-love. It seems more appropriate to the phenomenology of this stage to describe it as a state of primary nondifferentiation. It is only with the beginning of self-object differentiation that the question of primary self-love versus primary object-love becomes at all meaningful. But even here the controversy is rendered insubstantial by the functional conception of narcissism. The infant's newly differentiated self representation is highly vulnerable and fragile, lacking in cohesiveness and stable boundaries. Hence, the infant's earliest object relationships of necessity serve a basically narcissistic function—that is, they serve to consolidate the infant's rudimentary self representation. In other words, the earliest manifestations of the narcissistic function occur in relation to primary selfobjects, and the earliest object relationships serve a basic narcissistic function. Primitive object relationship and primitive narcissism are two sides of the same coin. The controversy regarding which came first is an artifact of the economic conception of narcissism and fades away when narcissism is understood in functional terms. Within the framework of a functional definition, narcissism as a developmental line pertains to stages in the growth of psychological structure that maintains the cohesion, stability, and positive affective coloring of the self representation. Growth proceeds from primitive prestructural narcissistic object relationships toward higher forms of narcissism by way of a gradual accretion of psychic structure which takes on the function of maintaining the self representation (Jacobson, 1964; Kohut, 1971, 1977; Tolpin, 1971).

4. Narcissism as Self-Esteem

Pulver's criticism of equating the drive concept of nar-

cissism (libidinal cathexis of the self) with self-esteem
(a complex cognitive-affective state) is worth quoting at
some length:

> . . . when the varying self images become organized into a
> more cohesive affective picture of the self, we speak of *self-
> esteem,* with "high self-esteem" implying a predominance
> of pleasurable affects and "low self-esteem" of unpleasur-
> able ones. All of these ego states of affect-self-representa-
> tion linkages may be either conscious, preconscious, or
> unconscious, have complex origins, and many defensive and
> adaptive functions.
>
> With all of this in mind, it should be clear that the
> proposition that self-esteem is simply the libidinal invest-
> ment of the self is woefully inadequate. It is an explanation
> of a complex ego state in drive terms, and very nonspecific
> drive terms at that. It not only precludes the consideration
> of the multiple factors determining self-esteem, but tries
> in an indirect way to explain affects by drives [1970, p. 334].

Pulver also cites the point made by Joffe and Sandler
(1967): that to explain self-esteem as the libidinal investment of the self introduces the economic notion that
self-esteem should decrease when a person becomes involved with objects and should increase when he with-
draws from objects and becomes self-absorbed. Obviously,
such a notion is not supported by clinical observations
that object relations can serve (with varying degrees of
success) to enhance self-esteem, and that the loss of object
ties can be catastrophic for it.

These conceptual difficulties are eliminated and the
relation between narcissistic activity and self-esteem is
clarified if the drive concept of narcissism is replaced by
the functional definition proposed here. Narcissism, as
functionally defined, is *not* synonymous with self-esteem,
which is conceived as a complex cognitive-affective state
multiply-determined by many factors. Narcissism embodies those mental operations whose *function* is to regulate self-esteem (the affective coloring of the self

representation) and to maintain the cohesion and stability of the self representation (the structural foundation upon which self-esteem rests). The relation of narcissism to self-esteem is analogous to the relation between a thermostat and room temperature. A thermostat is not equivalent to room temperature, nor is it the only determinant of room temperature. It is the function of a thermostat to regulate and stabilize room temperature in the face of a multitude of forces which threaten to raise or lower it. Similarly, self-esteem is vulnerable to the impact of a multitude of internal and external influences (see Jacobson, 1964). But when self-esteem is threatened, significantly lowered, or destroyed, then narcissistic activities are called into play in an effort to protect, restore, repair, and stabilize it. With regard to the point made by Joffe and Sandler, narcissism functionally defined as being in the service of self-esteem regulation is not incompatible with intense object relationships, which indeed may be in the same service.

5. *Narcissism as a Diagnostic Category*

The use of the concept of narcissism to refer to a diagnostic category originated in Freud's (1911b, 1914a) early distinction between the transference neuroses and the narcissistic neuroses. This diagnostic distinction, which was based on an evaluation of whether the principal target of libidinal investments was the object world or the self, partakes of the same conceptual difficulties and fallacies that have been shown to be inherent in the drive concept of narcissism. Furthermore, casting this diagnostic distinction in economic or energic terms led Freud and others to an unwarranted degree of therapeutic pessimism regarding the amenability of narcissistic disturbances to psychoanalytic treatment.

More recent diagnostic formulations place greater emphasis on the structural properties of self and object representations and the nature of the defensive organization than on the distribution of psychic energies. In this context, the diagnosis of "narcissistic personality disorder" has come into fashion.

According to Kohut (1971), patients with narcissistic personality disorders suffer from specific disturbances which are remnants of arrests in the development of the archaic grandiose self and/or the idealized parent imago. The clinical signs of narcissistic disorder are products of the failure of these primitive constellations to become integrated with the rest of the personality. In contrast to borderline and psychotic patients, those with narcissistic personality disorders have attained a cohesive (albeit archaic, grandiose, and vulnerable) self and have constructed cohesive, idealized parent imagoes, and therefore are not seriously threatened with the possibility of irreversible decompensations. In consequence of the attainment of these cohesive configurations, these patients are able to establish specific, stable narcissistic transferences. For Kohut, the spontaneous establishment of one of the stable narcissistic transferences, in which the analyst is relied upon as a mirroring or idealized selfobject rather than as a separate and whole object, is the best and most reliable diagnostic sign to distinguish patients with narcissistic personality disorders from those with transference neuroses, on the one hand, and from the borderline and psychotic cases, on the other.

While Kohut distinguishes sharply between narcissistic personality disorders and borderline conditions, Kernberg (1975, pp. 264-266) believes that narcissistic personality disorders are rooted in basically the same defensive organization, centering around splitting and allied defenses, that produces borderline psychopathology. Patients with narcissistic personality disorders differ from other, non-narcissistic borderline patients by virtue of possessing an integrated, though highly pathological grandiose self which reflects a defensive condensation of aspects of the real self, ideal self, and ideal object. The integration of this pathological grandiose self, which compensates for the lack of integration of the normal self-concept that is part of the underlying borderline organization, is responsible for the relatively good surface adaptation and social functioning of patients with narcissistic personality disorders. Hence, for Kernberg, the narcissistic personality disorder is a variant of the borderline condition, and the crucial diagnostic distinction is between borderline and psychotic organizations.

The functional concept of narcissism we are proposing brings considerable clarity to this diagnostic confusion. Within the proposed framework, "narcissistic disturbance" refers not to a diagnostic category, but rather to a *dimension of psychopathology* which cuts across all the traditional nosological entities.[2] Thus, one would speak of the *degree* of narcissistic disorder, referring to the degree of structural impairment and vulnerability of the self representation, the acuteness of the threat of narcissistic decompensation, and the motivational priority or urgency of the narcissistic function in a variety of pathological states. The degree of severity of narcissistic disturbance may be evaluated with reference to the three properties of the self representation included in the functional definition of narcissism—that is, its structural cohesion, temporal stability, and affective coloration.

In certain patients, the self representation is fre-

---

[2] This formulation seems to us to be consistent with trends in Kohut's later work (1977), in which the concept of a "narcissistic personality disorder" tends to be overshadowed by the broader concept of "self-pathology."

quently or predominantly negatively colored (feelings of low self-esteem), but is for the most part temporally stable and structurally cohesive. One might refer to such cases as mild narcissistic disturbances. In other patients, the self representation is frequently or predominantly negatively colored and, additionally, its organization is temporally unstable (experiences of identity confusion), but, notwithstanding temporary, reversible fragmentations, it largely retains its structural cohesion. One might refer to such cases as moderately severe narcissistic disturbances. In a third group of patients, the self representation is frequently or predominantly negatively colored, temporally unstable and, additionally, is lacking in cohesion and subject to irreversible structural fragmentation and disintegration (often signaled by spells of hypochondriasis, depersonalization, and derealization). One might refer to such cases as very severe narcissistic disturbances.

Thus, the functional concept of narcissism enables one to view narcissistic disturbance as a dimension of psychopathology that transcends traditional diagnostic categories and that can be assessed through an evaluation of the structural properties of the self representation and the degree of their impairment.

6. Healthy versus Unhealthy Narcissism

As Pulver points out, the drive concept of narcissism makes it difficult to differentiate pathological inflations of the self from a realistic good feeling about oneself because, with the drive concept, both are conceived as being due to the libidinal cathexis of the self. Indeed, it seems that the drive concept leads to the erroneous view that narcissism is by definition unhealthy since it exists at the expense of object attachments. In contrast, a functional definition of narcissism makes it possible to distinguish relatively unhealthy from healthy narcissism on the basis of the degree of structural impairment of the self representation, the acuteness of the threat of self-fragmentation, the motivational urgency of narcissistic reparative efforts, and the extent to which primitive, sexualized, and aggressivized selfobject configurations are relied upon for the restoration or maintenance of self-cohesion, self-continuity, and self-esteem. For instance, urgent attempts to maintain a fragile self representation through an archaic, sexualized tie to an idealized external object often fail, because such relationships tend to be subject to highly conflictual vicissitudes, and the state of the self representation will be highly vulnerable to the fate of the usually unstable relationship (Reich, 1953). On the other hand, the consolidation of a depersonified, internalized, and realistically tempered system of values and ideals provides a firm structural foundation for the maintenance of the self representation. As Jacobson (1964) points out, the development of such a system, which becomes relatively independent of external objects, contributes greatly to the stability of the self representation "which cannot be as easily affected as before by experiences of rejection, frustration, failure and the like," and to the successful maintenance of "a sufficiently high average level of self esteem, with a limited margin for its vacillations, apt to withstand to some extent psychic or even physical injuries to the self " (p. 132).

7. Countertransference

The drive concept of narcissism (and even the very term narcissism, which became enmeshed in the drive theory) can exacerbate the countertransference problems evoked in the analysis of narcissistic patients. The drive concept of narcissism as self-love may lead us to develop overt or covert rejective and contemptuous attitudes toward narcissistic patients insofar as it encourages us to view them as selfish, self-engrossed, and self-indulgent. As a result, we would tend to identify these patients with rejected aspects of our own selves or of our childhood objects. In contrast, a functional conception of narcissism helps to alleviate the countertransference problems that arise with narcissistic patients by enabling us to recognize that their narcissism is in the service of the survival of their sense of self. A functional orientation helps us to achieve empathy with such patients as we become engaged in understanding the purpose of their narcissistic activities and what has made them necessary. A functional definition helps us to accept primitive narcissistic attitudes as comprehensible and indispensable in view of a patient's level of development, and to endure our humble and at times thankless role in the narcissistic transferences of being nothing more than a selfobject—the embodiment of a function which the patient cannot yet perform himself (Kohut, 1971). And finally, an accurate functional understanding of narcissism helps us to avoid the sometimes countertransference-motivated pitfall of routinely interpreting narcissistic configurations as defenses against sexual and aggressive wishes toward objects (Oremland and Windholz, 1971).

SUMMARY

We are offering a critique of the traditional economic concept of narcissism as the libidinal investment of the self. We propose instead a functional definition, according to which mental activity is narcissistic to the degree that its function is to maintain the cohesion, stability, and positive affective coloring of the self representation. We further suggest that this functional conception of narcissism lends clarification to our understanding of the narcissistic perversion, narcissistic object relationships, narcissism as a developmental line, the relationship of narcissistic activity to self-esteem, narcissism as a diagnostic term, and the issue of healthy versus unhealthy narcissism. Finally, we contend that a functional understanding of narcissism can help analysts avoid certain countertransference pitfalls encountered with narcissistic patients.

3

The Narcissistic Function of Masochism

Traditionally, a theoretical symmetry has been maintained between narcissism and masochism. While narcissism had been defined as the libidinal cathexis of the self representation, masochism had been defined as its aggressive cathexis (Hartmann, 1950; Jacobson, 1964). A redefinition of narcissism thus demands a corresponding re-examination of masochism.

A review of the literature indicates that masochism is a complex, multifaceted phenomenon. It has been discussed as a normal element in the functioning of conscience (Brenner, 1959), as a fundamental capacity of the human mind to experience painful processes as pleasurable (erotogenic masochism), as a part of the sexual life of women, as a sexual perversion, and as a characterological pattern of behavior (the masochistic character, slavish submissiveness, moral masochism; see Stein, 1956; Loewenstein, 1957). Masochistic phenomena have been found to exist in a wide variety of clinical syndromes (Brenner, 1959; Panken, 1973). Additionally, masochism in its various manifestations has been interpreted as serving a number of different functions. It has been treated as an id phenomenon, i.e., as derivative of sexual and/or aggressive wishes which have undergone specific

28

vicissitudes at the various phases of psychosexual organization (Freud, 1919a, 1924; Fenichel, 1925, 1935; Nunberg, 1926; Deutsch, 1930b; Bak, 1946; de Monchy, 1950;
Gero, 1962). It has been viewed as a superego phenomenon, i.e., as arising from guilt and from the need to be
punished for forbidden desires (Freud, 1916, 1919a, 1924,
1928; Deutsch, 1930a; Dooley, 1941; Loewenstein, 1945).
And finally, it has been interpreted as an ego operation
or defensive maneuver, i.e., as a mode of relating to external and/or internal objects with the aim of warding off
various infantile danger situations and dreaded object
relations (W. Reich, 1933-1934; Horney, 1935; Berliner,
1947, 1958; Bergler, 1949; Menaker, 1953; Bieber, 1966;
Grand, 1973; Panken, 1973).

A ray of clarity was introduced into this maze of com-
plexity by Brenman's (1952) application of Waelder's
(1936) concept of the principle of multiple function to the
understanding of masochistic phenomena. Brenman cogently argued that the complexities of masochistic phenomena cannot be encompassed by any one of the three
structural concepts (id, ego, superego) alone. Brenman
viewed masochism as a complex configuration resulting
from the balancing of primitive unconscious sexual and
aggressive wishes, specific defensive processes, and specific creative or adaptive ego functions. She described
how one or another of these components might dominate
the manifest clinical picture, depending on the efficiency
of ego functioning (degree of decompensation) at any
given time. Brenman's illuminating integrative approach to masochism was later adopted and amplified in
important papers by Socarides (1958) and Brenner (1959).
The latter emphasized that a single set of masochistic
fantasies and behavior will serve a great variety of purposes in an individual, within the interplay of id, ego,
and superego functions.

Masochism, then, like other complex mental activities, is multiply determined and serves multiple functions. In this chapter we add to the already rich understanding of masochism by elucidating yet another function which masochistic phenomena may serve. We show that masochistic activities may, in certain instances, represent abortive (and sometimes primitively sexualized) efforts to restore and maintain the structural cohesion, temporal stability, and positive affective coloring of a precarious or crumbling self representation. According to the definition proposed in chapter 2, such efforts in the service of maintaining the self representation constitute the "narcissistic function" of masochistic manifestations. In order to round out our discussion, the narcissistic function of sadism, the contribution of narcissistic vulnerability to frustration-aggression, and the role of orgasm in the sadomasochistic perversions will also be considered.

The case material presented by a number of writers on masochism (Bak, 1946; Keiser, 1949; Bernstein, 1957; Bychowski, 1959; Eidelberg, 1959; Nydes, 1963; Kernberg, 1975; Bach and Schwartz, 1972; M'Uzan, 1973) indicates that florid masochistic activities frequently coincide with severe narcissistic pathology. Indeed, Keiser, and later M'Uzan, strongly implied that the masochist's primary anxiety is the dread of the structural dissolution of the self representation. The close association between masochistic phenomena and narcissistic pathology may also be inferred from developmental studies which traced the origins of severe masochistic tendencies to deprivations, traumata, and developmental interferences suffered in the early preoedipal years (Berliner, 1947, 1958; Keiser, 1949; Bergler, 1949; Menaker, 1953; Bernstein, 1957; Socarides, 1958; Bychowski, 1959; Panken, 1973). It is precisely during the earliest preoedipal era that the

infant is occupied with the developmental task of consolidating a rudimentary self representation which is
differentiated from the representations of his primary
objects (Jacobson, 1964; Mahler et al., 1975; Kohut,
1971). Hence, it seems safe to assume that the early
preoedipal traumata implicated in the origins of severe
masochism would also leave their mark by interfering
with the development of a cohesive and stable self representation. Indeed, Bergler (1949), Eidelberg (1959),
Bernstein (1957), Bychowski (1959), and Eisenbud (1967)
all claimed that early experiences of "narcissistic mortification" (severe injuries to the self representation) are
prerequisites for the development of masochism, and
Bernstein (1957) specifically pointed to the early developmental failure in masochistic patients to consolidate
a bounded self representation differentiated from primary object representations. And finally, analytic studies
of severely handicapped individuals (Freud, 1916; Bychowski, 1959; Jacobson, 1959) verify the close connection between severe narcissistic injuries and the
development of masochistic tendencies.

  The inference to be drawn, then, is that masochistic
activities, as *one* of their multiple functions, may serve
as abortive efforts to restore, repair, buttress, and sustain
a self representation that had been rendered vulnerable
by injurious experiences during the early preoedipal era,
when the self representation is developmentally most
susceptible to damage. This is not to argue that every
instance of masochism is primarily an attempt to maintain a precarious self representation. Indeed, the prominence of the narcissistic function will vary from one
masochistic individual to another, and from one masochistic activity to another within the same individual.
The notion of a "motivational hierarchy" (Rapaport,
1951) aids in the conceptualization of this issue. It may

be assumed that in the structurally intact psychoneurotic patient, the narcissistic function of sustaining the self representation will occupy a position of low priority in the motivational heirarchy of his masochistic tendencies. In such a patient masochism might, for example, primarily serve as an expression of guilt over unconscious oedipal wishes. On the other hand, in the structurally deficient patient with a fragile self representation, the narcissistic function will occupy a position of very high priority in the motivational hierarchy of his masochism. It is indeed in the structurally deficient personalities—the borderline and psychotic patients—that one consistently finds florid and primitive masochistic manifestations intermingled with severe pathology of the self representation (Bak, 1946; Bychowski, 1959; Nydes, 1963; Kernberg, 1975; Bach and Schwartz, 1972). Loewenstein (1957) alluded to the diagnostic significance of motivational priority when he distinguished the patient whose masochism was a "legacy of the Oedipus complex" from the patient whose masochism stemmed from severely defective ego functions.

In the remainder of this chapter we explore the various pathways along which the narcissistic function of maintaining the self representation is exercised through masochistic (and sadistic) activity.

THE NARCISSISTIC FUNCTION OF PAIN AND SKIN EROTICISM

In an individual with a diffuse or dissolving self representation, the masochistic search for acute experiences of pain can be understood as a means of acquiring a feeling of being real and alive (Panken, 1973) and thereby re-establishing a sense of existing as a bounded entity, a cohesive self. Such an inference is supported by the

finding that the masochist will often abandon the
sadomasochistic partnership when pain becomes disin-
tegrative rather than exhilarating (Keiser, 1949; Loewenstein, 1957). The masochistic quest for pain in the
structurally deficient individual may, then, represent a
desperate exaggeration of experiences in which a tem-
porarily disorientated person expresses the wish to be
pinched or slapped to affirm the reality of his self. In the
masochistic perversion the masochist may need the sen-
sation of acute pain to buttress his feeling of having a
cohesive self before he can risk the threat of self-loss
posed by sexual intimacy (Keiser, 1949). M'Uzan (1973)
described an extreme case of masochistic perversion in
which the patient sought grotesque experiences of pain
in order to restore self-boundaries and recover "narcissistic integrity" when his self representation was menaced. An analogous function of articulating and sustaining
the outlines of the self representation through real or
imagined pain may be served by beating fantasies
(Freud, 1919a; Joseph, 1965), and by the masochistic
provocation of symbolic beatings and psychic pain commonly found in moral masochists or masochistic char-
acters.

Similar considerations may apply to the exaggerated
"skin eroticism" frequently found in the masochistic
character (W. Reich, 1933-1934; Berliner, 1947, 1958;
Keiser, 1949; Loewenstein, 1957). Reich puzzled over the
question of why skin contact with a beloved person relieved anxiety in the masochist. Keiser provided a plau-
sible answer by speculating that the masochist is
specifically anxious about the intactness of his body because he has not been able to consolidate a stable and
integrated body image. The structurally deficient masochist, then, seeks erotic stimulation and warming of
the skin surface because it highlights the outlines of his

precarious body image and restores his sense of self-cohesion.

THE ROLE OF EXHIBITIONISM, THE AUDIENCE, AND THE MIRROR IN MASOCHISM

Numerous authors (W. Reich, 1933-1934; Reik, 1941; Fenichel, 1945; Berliner, 1947, 1958; Bergler, 1949; Eidelberg, 1959; Jacobson, 1959) have pointed out the exhibitionistic component in the masochistic character's demonstrations of suffering and martyrdom. In a structurally deficient individual, exhibitionism may be viewed as a primitive means of shoring up a failing self representation through eliciting a mirroring affirmation of the self from one's audience (Kohut, 1971; see the case of Mark, chapter 8). The presence of a real or imaginary audience to whom his misery can be dramatized seems to be a consistent requirement of the masochistic character (Brenman, 1952; Socarides, 1958). The specific content of the reponse which the masochist desires from the audience is variable. He may wish to force expressions of love and of his loveworthiness, of appreciation and approval, or of concern and sympathy. He may wish to punish his audience by evoking guilt feelings or remorse. Or he may wish to provoke his audience into giving him a symbolic beating. The common theme in all these variations is that he is not being ignored. By exhibiting his desolation he is being noticed, eliciting a response, having an *impact* on his audience. In one whose self representation threatens to dissolve, the experience of having the self reflected back and affirmed through his impact on a real or imaginary audience might add a desperately needed increment to his sense of self-cohesion. It is noteworthy in this regard that a number of masochistic patients described in the literature enacted their beating fantasies in front of a mirror (Joseph, 1965). These patients functioned as their own self-validating audiences.

MASOCHISM AND THE IDEALIZED PARENT IMAGO

Kohut (1971) has postulated that an individual who suffers from an absence of or defect in psychological structure that maintains the self representation may mobilize one of two primitive narcissistic configurations in an effort to solidify and sustain a sense of self-cohesion, self-continuity, and self-esteem. He may attempt to maintain a cohesive, stable, and positively colored self representation through merger with an aggrandized omnipotent selfobject ("idealized parent imago"). Or he may attempt to maintain his self representation through a selfobject who continuously mirrors back reflections of the individual's own archaic omnipotent wishful self ("grandiose self"). In either case a primitive narcissistic object relation substitutes for the missing or defective psychic structure which ordinarily maintains the self representation.

Several authors (Berliner, 1947, 1958; Menaker, 1953; Loewenstein, 1957; Socarides, 1958; Nydes, 1963) have developed the notion that the masochistic character stunts his own independent development, sacrifices his competence, and creates a debased and depreciated perception of his own self in order to sustain the image of an idealized, all-good, all-powerful maternal object on whom he can depend for nurture and protection. According to these authors, masochistic self-debasement in the service of object-aggrandizement functions to maintain an illusory but vitally needed dependent or symbiotic object relationship, and to ward off the aggression and resulting danger of object loss that would ensue if the patient were to recognize (rather than deny) the object's actual hatefulness and hostility. With regard to the theme of this chapter, the question arises whether the vitally needed object relation might in addition serve a narcissistic function in maintaining the self representation. In any given case, only careful clinical investigation (especially of the quality of the therapeutic relationship) can determine whether the masochist recognizes his partner as a separate object differentiated from his own self, or whether the masochist's object-hunger and dependency is due to the fact that merger with an idealized selfobject is striven for as a source of narcissistic sustenance and as a substitute for missing aspects of his own psychic structure (Kohut, 1971). The latter seemed to be the case for certain masochistic-submissive women described by A. Reich (1953) and Bernstein (1957). These women manifested a pattern of forming an enslaving narcissistic object tie to an aggrandized phallic ideal in order to undo the trauma of their imagined castration and the resulting sense of defect and inferiority. Union with the phallic ideal was sought as a magic method of repairing the damaged self representation and restoring injured self-esteem. Bychowski (1959), too, presented a series of predominantly borderline and psychotic patients, whose pattern of masochistic self-surrender was in the service of sustaining the imago of an idealized omnipotent parent, merger with whom (Bychowski used the term exchange) functioned largely to repair and reconstitute a traumatically shattered self representation. Bychowski's clinical illustrations suggest the speculation that the more closely and concretely the patient's masochism is drawn into the service of the primitive narcissistic configurations (idealized parent imago and grandiose self), the more the manifest clinical picture moves in the direction of overt paranoia. Bychowski's material also substantiates the notion that the more structurally deficient the patient, the more prominent is the narcissistic function in the motivational hierarchy of his masochism.

As a final example, Bach and Schwartz (1972), in their analysis of a dream and a series of perverse fantasies produced by the Marquis de Sade, concluded that the Marquis' primitive masochistic fantasies represented one pathway (the other pathway being through sadistic fantasies) along which he attempted to cope with acute narcissistic decompensation. The authors viewed de Sade's masochistic fantasies as regressive attempts to restitute and reanimate archaic idealized selfobjects, and interpreted the sexualization of these fantasies as a desperate effort to prevent experiences of self-fragmentation and self-dissolution.

MASOCHISM AND THE GRANDIOSE SELF

Masochistic activity may serve a threatened self representation not only by preserving the idealized parent imago, but also by creating a fantasied identity between the individual's actual self and his primitive grandiose wishful self. The masochist might, for instance, achieve an illusory feeling of omnipotence by identifying with his sadistic partner, vicariously participating in the latter's overt exhilaration of power (Freud, 1915; Reik, 1941; Eidelberg, 1959; M'Uzan, 1973). Or he might strive for the required omnipotence more directly, in the masochistic activity itself. Keiser (1949) pointed out that in the masochistic perversion the masochist achieves a sense of "complete control" over his punishment and his sadistic partner through an elaborate set of rules and regulations which stage the sexual situation as a "carefully planned play." Keiser (1949), Kohut (1971), and M'Uzan (1973) each discovered variations of a fantasy enjoyed by masochistic patients that in their perverse activities the sadistic partner would be weakened by his exertions and the masochist, the "victim," would emerge unscathed, thus proudly demonstrating his superior strength and affirming his omnipotence. Loewenstein (1957) emphasized the feelings of magical control and triumph over the dangers of punishment and rejection through a "seduction of the aggressor" which occurs in the masochistic perversion. He also noted the power dividend in the masochistic character's sulking. Similarly, Reik (1941), and later Eisenbud (1967), pointed out that behind the suffering of the masochistic character lurked fantasies of glorious "victory through defeat." Even suicide may represent a narcissistic triumph (Bach and Schwartz, 1972). Keiser (1949), Bernstein (1957), and Eidelberg (1959) all suggested that by actively producing his own failure and defeat and actively provoking humiliation, abuse, and punishment, the masochistic character experiences the illusion of magical control and triumphant power over his object world. Eidelberg (1959) argued that such illusions of magical control enable the masochist to deny his narcissistic vulnerability by retaining his fantasies of infantile omnipotence.

As with the reanimations of idealized object imagoes, careful clinical investigation must determine, for any given patient, the specific function of the illusory omnipotence embedded in his masochistic activities. In structurally deficient patients, such feelings of omnipotence may serve the narcissistic function of restoring or sustaining self-cohesion, self-continuity, and self-esteem by establishing a fantasied identity between the performance of the patient's actual self and his archaic grandiose wishful self.

Clinical experience suggests that in the well-compensated masochistic character, masochistic activity serves the self representation primarily by sustaining merger with the idealized parent imago, so that submissiveness, self-denial and self-surrender typify his relations with the object. However, when radical disillusionment, severe rejection, or abandonment by the object precipitates a decompensation of the masochistic equilibrium, the masochist may seek to restore his crumbling self representation by regressively reviving manifestations of the primitive omnipotent grandiose self (Kohut, 1971). Hence, in the decompensating masochistic character, narcissistic rage, hostile coerciveness, emotional blackmail and extortionist demands for love, and imperious and exhibitionistic expressions of unlimited entitlement to reparation and revenge may dominate the clinical picture (Brenman, 1952; Socarides, 1958). The structurally deficient masochistic character can renounce power for the sake of love (Nydes, 1963) only so long as there remains a thread of hope for merger with an idealized selfobject.

THE NARCISSISTIC FUNCTION OF SADISM

Sadism may function to restore a fragmenting self representation along pathways analogous to those followed by masochistic activity. The sadist may vicariously acquire a feeling of being alive and real through a process of identification with the acute pain he induces in his victim. Dramatically shocking and forcing attention from a real or imaginary audience through his cruelty may provide the sadist with a vitally needed experience of self-authentication. The sadist may also seek to restore in his victim the imago of an idealized, imperishable breast-mother, who patiently absorbs and survives the punishments he administers and who remains as a narcissistically sustaining presence despite his aggressions against her. And, finally, the sadist may seek self-cohesion in a feeling of identity with his archaic grandiose wishful self through an exhilarating exercise of extravagant power which creates an illusory sense of total omnipotent control over his masochistic partner (Bach and Schwartz, 1972; Fromm, 1973). Indeed, whereas the compensated masochist typically seeks narcissistic reparation by resurrecting the idealized parent imago, the structurally deficient overt sadist most commonly strives for self-cohesion, self-continuity, and self-esteem by attempting to revitalize and validate his grandiose wishful self. Though sadistic and masochistic tendencies are generally closely intermingled with one another (Brenner, 1959), the characterological predominance in a patient of overt sadism over masochism suggests an early massive disappointment by or absence of idealized primary selfobjects and a resultant reliance on the primitive grandiose self as a favored method of restoring and sustaining the damaged self representation (Kohut, 1971).

THE CONTRIBUTION OF NARCISSISTIC VULNERABILITY TO FRUSTRATION-AGGRESSION

The important role of aggression, both self-directed and object-directed, in sadomasochistic activities has been stressed by nearly every writer on the subject. Recent studies (Kohut, 1972; Rochlin, 1973) suggest that aggression is a peculiarly human response to narcissistic injuries, and may serve the individual's efforts to repair his damaged self representation. Indeed, one finds the most violent and primitive expressions of self-directed and object-directed aggression precisely in those individuals who are the most narcissistically vulnerable, i.e., who have the most fragile and precarious self representations. It may be assumed that for such people, a relatively minor frustration often represents a shattering narcissistic insult entailing the threat of self-fragmentation and self-disintegration. The primitiveness of such an individual's aggressive response to frustration is a measure of his extreme narcissistic vulnerability and the urgency of his need for narcissistic repair. It may be a breach of empathy in the treatment of a structurally deficient patient to make an issue of the hostile aggressiveness in his sadosmasochism rather than recognizing and appreciating with the patient the underlying narcissistic fragility and the desperate need for narcissistic restoration that make his primitive aggression necessary. With the structurally deficient patient, the analyst and patient must come to understand that the various forms of the patient's self-directed and object-directed aggression are in the service of the survival of his vulnerable self representation. Such an emphasis is a reaffirmation of Berliner's (1958) useful technical injunction that the analysis of the masochist as victim (his narcissistic vulnerability) takes priority over the analysis of the masochist as troublemaker (his hostile aggressiveness).

THE ROLE OF ORGASM IN THE SADOMASOCHISTIC PERVERSIONS

Nydes (1950, p. 306) characterized the orgasm as "a triumph of realization, which for an instant gives imminent life and power to the thoughts that surge on its crest." Similarly, Eissler (1958, p. 242) argued cogently that the experience of orgasm is "endowed with the power to confirm, create and affirm conviction," to provide the individual with a "conviction of truth" with regard to the reality of the images he is consciously or unconsciously entertaining at the moment of orgasm. Hence, the experience of orgasm in the sadomasochistic perversions (and other perversions as well) may give life to the accompanying fantasies and serve to restore ecstatically the structurally deficient individual's sense of conviction about the truth and reality of his having a bounded and cohesive self. (See chapter 8 for clinical illustrations). The degree of primitive sexualization (as with primitive aggressivization) of narcissistic reparative efforts is a measure of the degree of narcissistic vulnerability and the acuteness of the threat of narcissistic decompensation. The Janus-faced quality of the orgasm, in both offering the promise of self-articulation and posing the threat of self-dissolution (Keiser, 1949; M'Uzan, 1973), may account for the elaborate ritualization with which the structurally deficient individual must surround his perverse acts.

SUMMARY

We have explored several pathways along which masochistic (and sadistic) activity may be called into the service of the narcissistic function of restoring and sustaining the cohesion, stability, and positive affective coloring of a precarious, threatened, damaged, or fragmenting self representation. We suggest that the degree of structural deficiency and consequent narcissistic vulnerability of the individual will determine the motivational priority of the narcissistic function in his sadomasochistic activities, as well as the extent to which his narcissistic restorative efforts are primitively sexualized and aggressivized.

Part II

DEVELOPMENTAL PRESTAGES OF DEFENSES

4

The Ontogenesis of Denial

In the next three chapters we reformulate the concept of defense within a developmental framework. We propose that there is a developmental line for each defensive process, with precursors or *prestages* of the defenses occurring prior to the consolidation of self and object representations. Furthermore, we demonstrate that it is of utmost importance clinically to distinguish between mental activity that functions principally as a defense, warding off components of intrapsychic conflicts, and superficially similar mental activity that is more accurately understood as a remnant of an arrest at a prestage of defensive development characterized by deficiencies in the structuralization of the representational world.

The contribution of representational development to the formation of a defense is readily exemplified by the ontogenesis of denial, a prototypical defensive process which underlies many of the more complicated ones (A. Freud, 1936). In the present chapter, the psychoanalytic treatment of a young woman who lost her father when she was four years old will serve to illuminate the distinction between the defensive denial of an event and the prestages of denial which occur when the psychological structures necessary for accurate perception and assimilation of an event have not yet been consolidated. Con-

45

currently, it enables us to study the consequences for a girl of losing her father just before entering the oedipal phase.

The effects of the presence or absence of the mother during the early preoedipal period has dominated the analytic literature on child development and object loss (Spitz, 1965; Mahler et al., 1975), with particular emphasis on her contribution to the structuralization of self and object representations (Jacobson, 1964; Tolpin, 1971). Far less attention has been given to the effect on the child of the loss of the father. Losing either parent may trigger many consequences and collateral events. It is difficult, for example, to know whether developmental deviations should be attributed to the loss of the father or to a reactive change in the surviving mother and hence in the mother-child relation. The decisive factors in separating the effects of the traumatic loss of the father from the effects of its reverberations in the mother-child relation are conceptually important but clinically difficult to isolate. The case to be discussed demonstrates that such distinction may be drawn more clearly from the vicissitudes of the transference in the analytic situation.

The case stands in contrast to Fleming's (1972) findings with patients who had suffered an early object loss. Fleming emphasizes their inability to form attachments in adult life and their difficulty in forming a transference and in establishing a therapeutic alliance. Fleming did not investigate the differing effects of the loss of the father as compared to the loss of the mother, but writes of the "parent-loss patient" who, as a consequence of the loss, maintains an immature personality organization. In turn, this developmental interference with structuralization affects the quality of object relations.

Neubauer's (1960) review of the literature on the effects of object loss reflects the intensive study of the con-

sequences of maternal deprivation and loss of the mother
in the preoedipal years. No specific studies of reactions
to the loss of the father just before the oedipal phase and
its consequences in adult personality organization have
come to our attention. It might be expected, however,
that for the girl, the loss of the father just before oedipal
development might mar sexual and characterological
patterns of relating to men, the self-image, and sexual
identity, but leave relatively intact the structures derived from the preoedipal attachment to the mother.

Closely allied to the problem of object loss and most
germane to the ontogenesis of denial are the developmental prerequisites for the capacity to mourn. The age
at which the ability to mourn can be relied upon is placed
by Wolfenstein (1966) in adolescence. Certainly more
than the first four years are required. But it is unlikely
that every loss of a parent prior to adolescence is per-
manently debilitating without analysis. The ability of
the surviving parent to counter the denial of the loss, to
aid in the assimilation and acceptance of its reality, and
to serve as a model in the mourning process and for the
eventual termination of mourning plays a decisive role.

There is an inherent contradiction between conceptualizing the child's inability to accept the loss of a parent
as the result of denial and the view that mourning—and
hence the acceptance of the reality of a loss—requires the
successful mastery of certain developmental tasks. Does
the assimilation and acceptance of the reality of a loss
fail to occur because a defense is opposing it, or because
the young child has not yet developed the prerequisite
psychological structures for acknowledging the loss and
adapting to it? We propose a reconciliation of these contradictory views by distinguishing between denial as a
defensive process and the developmentally determined
inability to register or affirm an event, specifically the

inability to comprehend death, which we conceptualize as a *prestage* of denial. We are suggesting here a distinction between a relatively healthy child coping with an event for which he or she is developmentally (or structurally) unprepared, and a child already weakened by intrapsychic conflict, needing to defend against the perception of a particular reality that would evoke anxiety.

Denial as a defense has proven difficult to classify because of its overlap with and similarity to other defenses. Anna Freud (1936) considered it a primitive defense, while Moore and Rubinfine summarize the Kris Study Group's discussion of denial as follows: "Denial occurs in response to the ego's requirement that it reconcile reality to instinctual strivings and superego demands" (Fine et al., 1969, p. 53).

Jacobson (1971, ch. 4) has emphasized the distinction between denial and repression. The former deals with perceptions of reality whereas the latter deals with intrapsychic conflict. A difficulty remains, however, in that a perception of reality is subject to denial, especially when intrapsychic conflict is associated with that perception.

We suggest that the concept of denial be reserved for those situations in which the child's representational world may be expected to have matured sufficiently for him to acknowledge a reality—for example, the differences between the sexes—but he cannot do so because of the conflictual meanings, associations, or implications involved in that perception. In this example, denial as a defensive process would be instituted to ward off castration anxiety.

In certain instances, denial may arise as the second phase of a two-phase developmental process. In the first phase, a prestage of denial, the child strains to synthesize available information. The events with which he has to cope are beyond what would be considered the "average expectable environment" (Hartmann, 1939) and cannot be assimilated. His efforts to comprehend such traumatic events may entail the construction of fantasies which derive from his level of psychosexual development at the time of the events and which reflect both cognitive capacities and wish fulfillments. Under optimal conditions these fantasies change as the child's subjective world develops. They are not pathological unless they are used to ward off perceptions of reality and become static defensive structures. At that point the second phase, which we consider to be denial proper, comes into operation.

The realities a child must assimilate vary from the subtle nuances of its relation to the mother to vivid events involving exposure to sexual or aggressive scenes. Consequently, the age at which the child is expected to be capable of assimilating such events ranges from the preoedipal phase to adolescence, depending on the event. In the case of the death of a parent, it appears that at least the latency stage must be reached for the loss to be assimilated and accepted. A developmental framework is thus crucial for describing denial and distinguishing it from its developmental prestages.

The developmental inability to affirm an event occurs when the necessary psychological structures have not yet evolved. An event then becomes traumatic in that it is phase-inappropriate—for example, the loss of the father just before the oedipal phase. Such a loss not only coincides with the child's greatest need for the presence of the father, but also occurs when representational structures that would permit mourning have not yet become firmly consolidated.

The inability to acknowledge the reality of a loss may evolve into defensive denial when an appropriate model for mourning is missing and/or when the relationship to

the lost object was excessively ambivalent, and/or when
the meaning of the loss shifts because of external or developmental changes. All three factors applied in the case
of the patient to be discussed. In the years between the
loss of her father at the age of four and her realization
during latency of his probable fate, the patient constructed a variety of fantasies to account for his absence.
During and after latency, a qualitative shift occurred so
that the fantasies became static and served defensive
purposes.

The distinction we propose between the developmental inability to register or affirm the reality of an
event (prestage) and the defense of denial sheds light on
the so-called denial fantasies. Where denial is instituted
as a defense, the fantasy would reflect in an expectedly
static form the compromises of the psychosexual stage at
which it was constructed. In contrast, where the child is
developmentally unable to affirm an event such as the
loss of a parent, the fantasy becomes the heir of the lost
parent and may be expected to undergo the various psychosexual transformations to which the imago of the actual parent, were he alive, would be subjected.

The treatment of our patient is considered with specific reference to the psychosexual fantasies she constructed in reaction to the traumatic loss of her father
and the organization of these fantasies into a defensive
denial system. Thus, the case provides a clear illustration
of the evolution of a defense from its early prestages.

THE CASE OF ANNA

When Anna began her four-year analysis she was 31
years old. She had been married for twelve years and
worked as a real estate broker. She complained of both
diffuse anxiety and states of acute panic, the content of

which centered around fantasies that her husband would
leave her for another woman.

Anna was born in Europe where, in her early years,
she lived through the horrors of the second world war
and the Nazi occupation. When she was four years old,
her father was taken to a concentration camp where he
eventually died. During an analytic session, while exploring the ways in which she kept alive aspects of her
relationship with her father in her current experiences
with men, Anna made a startling discovery that proved
to be pivotal in her treatment. She suddenly realized that
she had never accepted the reality of her father's death.
Indeed, she exclaimed, she believed even now with a feeling of absolute conviction that her father was still alive.
Much of the remainder of her analysis was concerned
with uncovering the genetic roots and characterological
consequences of this firmly embedded conviction.

At age four Anna had not yet developed the cognitive
capacities which would have enabled her on her own to
comprehend the meaning of the terrible events that were
taking place around her, especially the sudden and
inexplicable disappearance of her father. The surviving
adults in Anna's environment, particularly her mother,
failed to provide sufficient assistance to her in the task
of assimilating the grim realities of the war and her
father's incarceration and death. Her mother falsified the
reality of the war, telling Anna that the exploding bombs
were just doors slamming. She also pretended to Anna
that her father was not taken to a concentration camp
and tacitly perpetuated the myth that he was alive by
never directly discussing his death with Anna and never
openly mourning his loss. These experiences left Anna
with a feeling of confusion about what was real and what
was unreal, a feeling that was reanimated in her analysis
with the discovery of her unconscious conviction that her

father was still alive. It was left to Anna's own fantasy life to fill the vacuum left by maternal omissions and falsifications in order to make some sense of these incomprehensible and tragic events and to regain some feeling of comprehension and mastery: "I had to find some reason. It all seemed so crazy. I couldn't accept that such things could happen and there was nothing you could do. I was trying to understand what was happening. None of the adults would tell me. No one sat down with me and told me my father was in a concentration camp or dead. So I made up my own explanations."

The specific content of the fantasies which Anna elaborated to "explain" her father's disappearance and continued absence developed as the complex consequence of several factors, including her level of cognitive development, the particular circumstances surrounding her father's disappearance, the nature of her relationship with her father, and her psychosexual organization at the time of his loss.

With regard to cognitive development, there is evidence that a child at age four has not yet attained the abstract concept of death as a final and irreversible cessation of life (Nagy, 1959; Stolorow, 1973). To the extent that a death is acknowledged at all, it is typically conceived of as a potentially reversible departure to a distant geographical location. A common element in all of the conscious fantasies with which Anna explained her father's absence was the notion that he was living somewhere in a distant land and might some day return to her. Throughout her childhood and on into adulthood, at first consciously and later unconsciously, she "waited and waited" for him to come back to her and feared that she might "miscalculate" or "do something wrong" that would make her miss her "last chance" to see him.

Consistent with this level of cognitive and moral development, Anna, in her fantasy explanations, blamed herself for her father's departure and continued absence. The particular circumstances surrounding his departure contributed to the content of her fantasies. Anna recalled that she had found a notice and had brought it to her father. She did not understand what it was and took it very lightly. She even felt excited about the opportunity to deliver something to her father. When she gave the notice to him, she danced around him in a very happy and excited mood. Later she came to believe that the notice had instructed him to report to the Nazi authorities, and she felt she had done a terrible thing to him by being so happy. After he was gone, she developed a fantasy that he hated her for being happy when she delivered the notice because her happiness meant she did not care about him. She further fantasized that had she demonstrated her love and devotion by becoming "hysterical enough" about the notice, he would have returned to her: "He stayed away because I was such a rotten little kid to have acted happy, and he was glad to be away from me. If only I had given him a proper farewell. I missed my last chance to make him want to come back."

Thus Anna imagined that her father's continued absence was a kind of retribution for her complacency in taking the notice and his departure so lightly. As an older child, to the extent that she became dimly aware of the tortures he must have experienced in the concentration camp and, later, of his death, she continued to blame herself. She imagined that if she had not delivered the notice or if she had been miserable, upset, and hysterical enough when she delivered it, her father would have been magically spared. In the transference whenever she was faced with a separation from the analyst, Anna revived these elements of her fantasy. On such occasions she worked herself up into a state of acute panic and frenzied worrying as a kind of "ritual sacrifice" in order to "prevent disaster"—to insure that the temporary separation would not turn into a permanent one as it had with her father when she had been so complacent.

The guilty, self-blaming elements in Anna's fantasy explanations must of course be placed within the context of her relationship with her father at the time of his departure. Anna recalled that she loved her father dearly, but that her boundless love for him had been only partially requited. He was often away on long business trips and was sometimes preoccupied, irritable, distant, and rejecting of her affectionate overtures and demands for attention. At times Anna felt hurt and left out because her father and mother were very devoted to each other and often went out together, leaving her behind. On occasion Anna had a guilty wish to be "relieved" of the strain of the thrilling but sometimes painful "game" of trying to win expressions of love from her father. Clearly, to the extent that her great love for him had been disappointed and rebuffed, she had harbored angry wishes to be rid of him. When he was taken away, her feeling of guilt contributed to the content of her self-blaming fantasies.

The final elements for Anna's fantasy explanations of her father's disappearance—perhaps the most fateful ones for her characterological development—were provided by the vicissitudes of her psychosexual development. Because her father had been taken away when she was four years old, Anna's explanations of his absence included features of both the castration anxiety period and the oedipal stage. She developed fantasies that her father stayed away because she was defective, repulsive, and totally valueless to him. And she developed further fantasies that he stayed away because he had met another woman and had chosen to stay and live with her:

if Anna could just win him away from the woman who had stolen him, he would return.

Material that unfolded in the course of her analysis suggested that castration imagery played the more prominent role in her interpretation of her father's absence. The loss of her father intensified and magnified the feelings of mortification and self-devaluation characteristic of the castration-anxiety phase, because this was a time when Anna had turned to her father as an idealized self-object (Kohut, 1971, 1977) in whose phallic grandeur she could share and thus regain a feeling of wholeness and self-worth. The father Anna had lost was not primarily the sexual father-as-lover of the fully blossomed oedipal phase; rather, he was the strong, powerful, glorious, presexual father-as-protector of the phallic phase from whom she sought shelter against a threatening world, reparation of her narcissistic wounds, and a sense of having value. The importance of castration feelings in Anna's reaction to the loss of her father was evidenced both by her pattern in adult life of forming attachments to powerful, protective phallic father-figures and by the important role that a distinct illusory penis played in her development. From her early childhood, Anna had maintained a fully conscious conviction that a small penis protruded from between her vaginal lips, a conviction which held disastrous consequences for her developing self-image and sense of sexual identity.

Although the exact time at which the illusory penis crystallized could not be established, it can be fairly safely assumed that its rudiments appeared as a direct response to her father's disappearance. The illusory penis is subject to two complementary explanations. According to the first, Anna imagined that her father stayed away because her defective and "castrated" genital made her disgusting and valueless to him: she was "only a girl," she had no penis. She then developed the fantasy of possessing a penis in an attempt to repair her imagined defect and as an expression of her wish to make her father value her and return to her now that she was "whole." However, the penis fantasy only exacerbated her feelings of defectiveness. Later in life Anna made further efforts to repair her "defect" by forming ties to aggrandized phallic father-figures, union with whom would undo her imagined castration.

According to the second explanation, the penis fantasy was an attempt to restore her father by enshrining a part of him in her own body image. She developed the illusory penis to make restitution for the loss of the whole object by incorporating a highly valued part object, her father's penis. Indeed, the tenacity with which she later clung to her illusory penis was paralleled only by the tenacity with which she maintained her conviction that her father was still alive.

The various explanatory and restitutive fantasies discussed so far cannot technically be described as defensive denial fantasies. Primarily, they represent attempts on the part of a four-year-old child to adapt to a state of cognitive and structural insufficiency; that is, to fill in with phase-specific fantasy elaborations the vacuum left by an immature psyche inadequately supported by the surviving adults in her environment. Hence, we would refer to these fantasies as a prestage of denial.

At some point after the war, during her latency period when cognitive and emotional maturation and expanded sources of information had enabled Anna to begin to register and comprehend the realities of her father's incarceration and death, she indeed began to construct an elaborate defensive denial-in-fantasy system (see A. Freud, 1936; Fleming, 1972), which, until its dissolution by analysis, functioned to keep her father alive. Her efforts at this later time can properly be described as a denial that prevented the mourning process of which she was now becoming developmentally capable. The denial was promoted by the multiple components of her complex, ambivalent attachment to her father. She wished to keep him alive because she wanted to spare him a horrible death and also to keep alive the hope that he would return and she would again enjoy his love. She wished to keep him alive because she felt terribly guilty and magically blamed herself for his death. And she wished to keep him alive because she needed once again to feel sheltered by his protection and united with his phallic grandeur.

In constructing the denial-in-fantasy system, Anna made ample use of the ready-made fantasies by which she originally had explained her father's absence. In order to deny his death, she now had to cling to both the castration imagery and fantasies of oedipal defeat. And to maintain this denial system, she had to select and cling to negative memories of her father's devaluing, rejecting, and excluding her—and repress all positive memories of his loving, caring for, and valuing her, lest they contradict and jeopardize her denial fantasies. The repressed, split-off imago of the good, loving father was displaced to the memory of a kindly uncle to whom Anna attributed gifts from her father and other expressions of his love. In adult life, Anna further buttressed her denial system by clinging to real or imagined experiences in which a father surrogate would devalue or reject her or would leave her for another woman. This, in turn, supported her conviction that her father was rejecting of her or chose another woman but was still alive. Furthermore, she warded off experiences of feeling loved, valued, or chosen by a man so that her denial fantasies and her devotion and loyalty to her father would not be jeopardized. Clearly, when Anna's denial fantasies coalesced into a static defensive system that had to be maintained at all costs, it had extremely deleterious consequences for her self-esteem as a woman as well as for her characterological patterns of relating to men.

It was between the age of ten and early adolescence that circumstances necessitated the final solidification of Anna's denial fantasies into a static and unassailable system. When Anna was ten her mother remarried, and Anna's denial fantasies dovetailed with a host of oedipalcompetitive and sexual conflicts, greatly intensified and complicated by her hope that her stepfather would substitute for her lost father. At this point Anna, in reality a bright and pretty child, began to feel ugly, stupid, defective, and "freaky" and became obsessively preoccupied with her illusory penis—symptoms which remained with her until they were removed by the analysis.

These castration themes served multiple functions for Anna during this crucial period in her development. The oedipal triad quickly evolved into a highly dangerous situation in which her stepfather openly expressed a preference for Anna and met her blossoming sexual fantasies and provocativeness with overt seductiveness. Her mother, an insecure, subservient, masochistic woman, was an inadequate oedipal rival who promoted rather than discouraged the developing sexual bond between Anna and her stepfather. Quite consciously and deliberately, Anna used her feeling of defectiveness and the illusory penis to avert the dangerous possibility of overt sexual activity with her stepfather, reassuring herself that he would not want her once he discovered her "deformity." Feeling and acting as if she were ugly and stupid prevented a dangerous oedipal victory. It served to pacify her mother and to insure Anna against being deserted by or destroying her. The various castration themes became gifts of love which preserved her mother and elicited her regressively needed nurturance. The illusory penis also served Anna's wish to compete with her stepfather for her mother's love, as well as her struggle to disidentify with her mother's subservient, masochistic qualities.

Additionally, feeling ugly, stupid, and undesirable to her stepfather warded off Anna's wish—and averted the possibility—that her stepfather would become a father substitute and thus intrude into and jeopardize her deep bond of devotion and loyalty to her real father. Anna felt ugly, was self-hating, and developed talionic dreams of being buried alive, partly because she felt tempted to commit her mother's crime of burying her real father by accepting her stepfather as a replacement.

Her mother's remarriage represented to Anna the first tacit acknowledgment of her father's death by the adults in her environment. This threatened abruptly to obliterate her denial fantasies. Anna was thus forced to redouble her efforts at denial and restitution and to fortify all the mental operations by which she was keeping her father alive: feeling defective, freaky, and worthless; brooding over her illusory penis; and imagining that boys would reject her and prefer other girls. Moreover, she had to mobilize feelings of being totally unloved and abused by her stepfather, because to recognize and accept his affection and caring would mean accepting that her father, too, had loved and valued her and was therefore absent because he was dead. By fending off her stepfather with castration imagery, Anna not only protected herself and her mother from the dangers of oedipal competition, she also insured that she would not "miscalculate" by accepting her father's death and accepting her stepfather. She insured as well that she, unlike her mother, would be ready and waiting for her father when he returned.

The final solidification of her denial system occurred during Anna's early adolescence as her pubertal development exacerbated the threat of overt sexual activity with her stepfather. In response to her stepfather's sexual intrusiveness and seductiveness, Anna would think to herself, "My real father would never do such things," and she wistfully yearned for her real father's return. She elaborated fantasies in which he would return, her mother would choose to stay with the stepfather, and Anna would remain with her real father and enjoy his care and protection. Anna, like Freud's Dora (1905a), called upon the imago of the idealized protective father to rescue her from a sexual threat. This necessitated the final cementing of her denial fantasies, through which she kept her father alive, into a static defensive system with all its unfortunate consequences for her self-image, self-esteem, and patterns of relating to men.

Much of this history was of course recapitulated in the transference. During the period when the analytic work consisted of active confrontations with the denial fantasies and encouragement for Anna to accept the reality of her father's death, she became immersed in rage-filled transference struggles in which she cast the analyst in the image of the sexually intrusive stepfather who threatened to destroy her devotion and loyalty to her real father.

The therapeutic alliance withstood the impact of these transference storms, and Anna was eventually able to work through the transference and to give up her denial system. The most immediate consequence was that she experienced a belated mourning process as she permitted herself to imagine the tortures and horrible death her father must have suffered at the hands of the Nazis. (At this point she also began to fear that the analyst would die.) Coincident with this unfolding mourning process was Anna's dramatic recovery of positive memories of a loving father; along with these memories, she also retrieved repressed memories of loving devotion from various other men. Anna now clearly recognized that she had elaborated a complex denial system in which she viewed herself as defective and sacrificed her memories of her father's and other men's love in order to spare her father the terrible, agonizing death she now realized he must have experienced. Just as the sacrifices she endured to keep him alive were a measure of her great love for her father, so now was her pain in belatedly imagining how he died.

As Anna accepted and mourned the death of her father, she also began to give up her feelings of being defective and undesirable. The working through of her denial system and her father's death had made possible the uncovering and reintegration of the repressed, split-off imago of a loving father. This in turn resulted in marked and lasting improvements in her self-image and self-esteem and in increasingly strong feelings of being valued and desired by men in her current life. Since she no longer needed to use certain castration themes and experiences of oedipal defeat to deny her father's death, she could return in her analysis to residual castration and oedipal conflicts and begin to resolve them in their own right.

SUMMARY

We have presented the case of a young woman whose neurotic personality structure evolved from the trauma of the death of her father when she was four years old. The loss of her father during her transition from the period of castration anxiety to the oedipal phase eventuated in specific disturbances in her self-image, her sexual identity, her self-esteem, and the pattern of her relationships with men. However, as evidenced by her capacity to maintain a therapeutic alliance during difficult transference struggles, the loss had not obliterated the stable and differentiated self and object representations which reflected the developmental achievements of the relatively benign years before her father's death. Hence, for Anna, the loss of her father affected the content and affective coloration of self and object representations but did not interfere with their structuralization.

The case provided a clinical illustration of the theoretical distinction between failure to register and affirm the reality of a loss because of cognitive and structural immaturity and inadequate support by the surviving adults (prestage of denial) and the defensive denial of a loss. At age four, Anna had been developmentally incapable of comprehending the death of her father, and the fantasies with which she attempted to explain his absence became the heir of the lost father and underwent the psychosexual transformations to which the imago of the actual father would have been subjected had he been alive. Hence her explanatory fantasies were shaped by her psychosexual organization at the time of the loss. Later, when circumstances made it necessary, Anna, who was now developmentally capable of assimilating her father's death, wove these explanatory fantasies into a denial system proper—a static system which had to be buttressed at all costs by various secondary defensive operations and supporting fantasies. This defensive system constituted the nucleus of Anna's neurotic personality structure. Its discovery and dissolution were pivotal to her analysis, making possible a belated mourning process and lasting improvements in her self-image and self-esteem.

5

Idealization and Grandiosity

The analyses of two patients with narcissistic pathology offer an opportunity to reconstruct the differing origins and meanings of their idealizations and grandiosity and thus to broaden our study of the role of psychic structuralization in the formation of defenses. For one patient idealizations and grandiosity were predominantly manifestations of a developmental arrest at a prestage of defense; for the other, predominantly defenses against intrapsychic conflict. We attribute differences in the function of idealizations and grandiosity in these two patients to the role of aggression and to the degree of intrapsychic separation attained.

In the previous chapter, we attempted to clarify the concept of denial by placing it within a developmental framework. We proposed a distinction between the defensive denial of an event, on the one hand, and the developmental inability to register and affirm its reality, on the other. We now extend this developmental framework to a consideration of the nature of idealizations and grandiosity. Idealizations may be viewed as a special category of failures to perceive reality accurately. When the self or an object is idealized, real qualities are inaccur-

ately recognized or acknowledged (see Schafer, 1967). We
propose a distinction, analogous to that made in regard
to denial, between idealizations based on a developmental inability to register and affirm the real qualities
of the self or objects (prestage of defense), and idealizations in which there is a defensive denial of the real
qualities of the self or objects. We follow the convention
of referring to idealizations of the self as grandiosity.

When idealizations based on a developmental inability to register and affirm the real qualities of the self or
objects appear in an adult, they indicate structural deficiency and an arrest in development whereby adequate
self-object differentiation and self and object constancy
have not been reliably attained. An example is the individual who has remained arrested at and vulnerable
to regressions to primitive, prestructural narcissistic self-
object configurations (Kohut, 1971). By contrast, with
idealizations involving defensive denial, sufficient differentiation and structuralization have occurred for accurate recognition and acknowledgment of real qualities
of the self or objects. However, archaic idealizations are
retained and consolidated into a static defensive system
that functions to ward off perceptions of those real qualities of the self or objects which are associated with anxiety and intrapsychic conflict. An example is the individual
who reactively idealizes himself and/or objects lest recognition of their real qualities evoke dangerous conflicts
over aggressive wishes (see Jacobson, 1964; Kernberg,
1975).

Our two cases illustrate the distinction proposed
above. By examining the treatment implications of this
distinction, we attempt to show that the proposed distinction can reconcile the opposing views that have arisen
concerning the nature and treatment of narcissistic disturbances (Kohut, 1971; Kernberg, 1975; Spruiell, 1974).

IDEALIZATIONS AND GRANDIOSITY BASED
ON A DEVELOPMENTAL ARREST

At the time Jane began her five-year analysis she was 27 years old. Although her primary complaint was her inability to complete her Ph.D. dissertation in American literature, a long history of complaints soon emerged which had as their common core a difficulty in self-esteem regulation. Even the writing block, so frequently the culmination of an oedipal conflict (which indeed was not absent), was better understood as an outgrowth of her narcissistic disturbance.

At the start of her analysis, Jane used her inability to complete her dissertation as clear evidence of her essential inadequacy: she was made of "flawed, unredeemable goods." The exploration of this material led to several interrelated lines of association. First, there was a conflictual relation with her mother, who, during the patient's latency years, never fulfilled her own writing aspirations in deference to her duties as a mother. Furthermore, an intense symbioticlike attachment still remained between mother and daughter, in which the patient received instructions from her mother on how to "fix" troublesome situations. Generally, her mother emphasized some behavioral change so that an appearance of acceptability could be maintained. Independent experience by the patient carried with it a threat of separation and had to be undone. Jane would report important events of her life to her mother which would become real to Jane only in the telling. Hence, she needed her mother as a selfobject to validate her experience.

A second line of associations led to an analysis of the work problem. In this context the patient described the meaninglessness of work for her. She recalled that when she was an adolescent, her parents had decided that she and her younger brother should "do chores" in the house. Her assignment was to place the salt and pepper shakers on the table before dinner. If by chance the housekeeper had already set them on the table, they had to be removed so that Jane could fulfill her assignment.

While there were earlier prototypes for the meaning of work, the implications here were apparent. Work was inconsequential and unnecessary. These associations eventually led to an explication of her relationship with her father. She recalled that her father's expressed attitude had always been great satisfaction that he could provide so well for the family financially, and that he could spare them the struggles which characterized his climb up the corporate ladder. He told both children that he wanted to spare them "from having to grovel at the foot of the mountain" and wished to "whisk them up to the top of the mountain by helicopter."

An event that became a focal point for Jane's psychopathology occurred at age seven when she was sent to ballet class to "cure" her of her "overweight" and to give her "grace." She returned home from the class one day in her leotards, looking forward to showing her father how delicately she could float across the living room. When her father returned home that evening she immediately performed for him. He let slip the comment, "Nothing helps."

The impact of this experience was profound. It accelerated a social withdrawal, with trancelike fantasy states used as a buffer against both real success and anticipated failure. Her joyful exhibitionism was depleted by the traumatic rebuff, shattering her self-esteem, while grandiose strivings were repressed. The experience served to strengthen the regressive tie to her mother, while an implicit "contract" was made with her father: she would suppress all evidence of anger, disappointment, criticism, or general displeasure with him if he would refrain from verbalizing how disappointed he was in her appearance.

These themes reveal aspects of the work block which are based on oedipal conflicts: the fear of surpassing her mother by triumphing in an area of painful failure for her and the wish to please her father by maintaining him in the position of financier. They also shed light on the origins of her narcissistic vulnerability. It is with respect to the latter that the material which proved crucial to the analysis of the work block will be considered.

At the age of fourteen, Jane spent the first of several summers in a camp where she found herself among the "attractive, brilliant, artistic, sensitive, slender, graceful people," any one of whom she felt her parents would have preferred as their daughter. The friends she made there and retained were endowed with idealized qualities she believed she could never attain. Through proximity to these friends she hoped to be included in their "glow." Her idealization of them gave her the feeling that although she was unacceptable, at least her values were ennobled. Though she could not compete in their "league," she was at least in the "right ball park." She had a keen sense of being included on a trial basis and attempted to ensure her tenous inclusion through self-devaluation, "currying favor," and ingratiation. Her self-esteem clearly fluctuated with every nuance of the reactions of these friends to her. She was subject to profound states of humiliation and depression which were covered socially with a forced "bonhomie" and a brilliant wit, and privately by overeating and the trancelike states filled with dreams of glory. The relationships formed here embodied remnants of archaic idealizations and repressed grandiosity.

The analytic exploration of the manner in which Jane attempted to work on her dissertation brought to light the specific deficiencies that produced the work block. To write her thesis required an "immersion" in work which threatened the tie to her idealized friends. The "hot line" to them, either in person or by telephone, served a vital narcissistic function. It prevented a dreaded disintegration of her self representation. When these contacts were disrupted, as in periods of work, she became depressed and attempted to restore her endangered self representation by eating compulsively, sleeping excessively, and becoming preoccupied with her appearance and weight. Fantasies and memories of slights and humiliations plagued her and reinforced the conviction that she was "basically unredeemable." Renewed contact with her friends could momentarily rescue her from these oppressive feelings and reinstitute a self-image which gained a more positive tone—"gilt by association." The rise in self-esteem was precarious, however, because it was accompanied by self-devaluation for being so dependent upon and vulnerable to others. So long as the regulation of self-esteem was in the hands of others—substitutes for missing self-regulating structure—independent solitary work was impossible. To be alone threatened her self representation with disintegration.

The dissertation itself was drawn into the narcissistic disturbance as well. It had become the heir of the grandiose "ballet" fantasy of childhood. The repressed exhibitionistic wishes of childhood reappeared in her vain hope of redeeming herself by writing "The Great American Dissertation." The archaic nature of her grandiosity showed itself in the majestic and unbridled nature of her thesis plan. Her grandiose expectations defied fulfillment and enforced a constant confrontation with her "inadequate abilities."

The history and the narcissistic disturbance that have been described permit a conceptualization of the role of idealization in Jane's life. Throughout her childhood, she never felt an absence of love from her parents, but rather a lack of admiration and respect and a very specific failure of empathy. She maintained an overtly dependent relationship with her mother, who also functioned as an idealized selfobject whose presence was necessary to validate, judge, and "fix" her experience. Her mother's role or capacity to perform this function was never challenged. Although geographical separation from her mother was accomplished, her role as a substitute for missing psychic structure was relegated to various surrogates. Their presence gave her life meaning and her self a momentary sense of cohesion, continuity, and positive affective coloration.

Because the patient had been referred for analysis by the therapist of one of her idealized friends, the halo was quickly placed upon her analyst. The transference which evolved absorbed the symbioticlike tie to her mother. Telling the analyst her experiences gave them meaning. The fact that the analyst offered neither judgments nor advice (what the patient described as her mother's "cosmetic suggestions") served as a sufficient contrast against which to explore her need for her mother as a structure substitute.

Although both parents seemed to be competent, outgoing, independently functioning people, leaders in their respective fields of interest, the enduring impression within the family was quite different. Jane described her father as "uninvolved," hiding behind his newspaper at night, a romantic but mysterious figure who knew the world, believed no one in his family could survive in it without his help, and prided himself on his ability to shield his "loved ones" through his power and wealth. She portrayed her mother as unfulfilled and forever currying favor—"a popularizer of ideas" who espoused liberal causes and views but couched them in terms that would not offend anyone. Differences within the family were glossed over, and feelings of anger, when evoked, went unacknowledged.

Jane consciously remembered feeling a lack of admiration, an "essential humiliation" within the family, even prior to the ballet episode. This incident did not stand alone, but was typical of experiences which deflated and suppressed the grandiose self prematurely and embodied empathic failures which in turn interfered with the structuralizations required for autonomous self-esteem regulation.

Jane was able to assuage the resulting feelings of inadequacy and worthlessness, her "basic unacceptability," with signs of acceptance from her idealized friends or with a "good" conversation with her mother. Analytic exploration of this method of restoring self-esteem led to the uncovering of her "lying": glossing over or withholding differences of opinion and values from these friends or voicing feigned agreement with them in an attempt to remain in their good graces. She was afraid of being alienated from them if she said no to their demands or appeared "ungraceful," and she accepted a "slave" status in order to bask in their artistic aura. Feelings of resentment or annoyance she quickly rationalized, so that any "unpleasantness" was her "fault."

Through her associations in the analysis Jane recalled a "religious" period between ages eleven and thirteen. This was preceded by feelings of envy of her mother's attractiveness and angry feelings toward both parents. When Jane learned that a neighboring couple were killed in an automobile accident, she became fearful that her parents would be killed in this manner. Thereupon she made a deal with God: if her parents would return home safely that evening, she would become a devotee. Their safe return ushered in an intense ritualistic, religious period which ended as abruptly as it had begun. When Jane asked her mother if she believed in God, her mother hesitated before responding; Jane interpreted this as a "no." Thus, when Jane's obsessive-compulsive defense against hostility toward and envy of her mother threatened to become divisive, it was quickly relinquished, and she began to emulate her mother's atheism. Clearly, her need to sustain the symbioticlike attachment to her mother far outweighed both Jane's hostility and her defense against it. The symbioticlike, confessional relationship continued into adulthood and was given additional impetus each time a new developmental task threatened to interrupt it. For example, in college when Jane was attracted to a young man, she sought and received her mother's blessing to have sexual relations with him. In the analysis, Jane's assertion, "When my mother gets hurt, I feel it," gave testimony to the extent to which self-object differentiation had been arrested.

In the analysis, Jane revived the specific period following her rebuff by her father (the ballet incident). At times her relationship with the analyst was indistinguishable from a continuation of the close tie to her mother in which boundaries were obliterated and all "secrets" confessed. This symbioticlike bond, intensified during the latency years, obviously also contained the preoedipal attachment to her mother, the revival of which occasioned phase-appropriate strivings for separation. In the treatment situation this was manifested in Jane's wish to know more about the analyst, especially his views on certain current political and social issues. She claimed that she had to know where he stood to be able to trust him. Until that point, she said, she was grateful that he had not intruded his opinions into her life as her mother had done, but had given her a nonjudgmental counterpart to her own tendency toward harsh, self-critical views. What looked like a frequently encountered resistance was actually, at this point, in the service of separation. The request that the analyst assert his individuality reflected the emergence of a developmental step. The burden of separation, however, was still placed on the analyst rather than on herself. When this was interpreted to her she took it as evidence of respect for her individuality. The analysis continued, and the initial request did not need to be fulfilled.

The revival of her feeling that she was merged with, engulfed by, and defined by her mother was accompanied by a sense of hopelessness and discouragement about the slowness of the analytic process. During this phase the transference began to shift. She began to see the analyst as the uninvolved father whom she might seduce into admiration of her. Early in this transitional phase she described a vignette from her work as a teacher: interviews with two of her students, both of whom were personally very troubled about their poor academic work. Against the background of her complaints about the lack of help she was getting in her analysis, she described the help she was able to give her students in a half-hour interview with each one. The analyst's response here required an assessment of the extent to which a narcissistic transference still held sway, because an empathic failure by him might repeat the "ballet incident" trauma in the treatment situation. The analyst therefore reflected back to Jane the pride and pleasure she took at having helped her students—and stopped at that. At a later point in treatment she was able to return to this incident and deal with the implicit competitive aspects.

Jane reacted to the uncovering of the repressed grandiose fantasies about her dissertation with shame at her grandiosity and self-criticism for her unrealistic expectations. She saw her "narcissism" as "immoral" and herself as a "spoiled, demanding, gluttonous child." To avoid the embarrassment of another humiliating "ballet" performance, she concluded that the only alternative would be to settle for a thoroughly pedestrian work. She now saw the analysis as a process which would force her to accept her "hopeless, inadequate, flawed self" and to relinquish all hope of admiration. The "vertical split" in the psyche, described by Kohut (1971), is exemplified here, and the therapeutic approach began by spelling out the dilemma: how to maintain the creative aspects of her original grandiose plan and to form a partnership between the grandiosity and the more realistic perception of her limitations, thereby harnessing the grandiosity in the service of realistically feasible and satisfying goals. Spelling out this dilemma avoided the dangers of moralizing about her narcissism and viewing it merely as pathology that had to be eliminated (a "cosmetic solution"). Spelling out the dilemma also enabled her to arrive at an acceptable compromise in which she added certain limitations without yielding on the novel aspects of her contribution.

The transformation of the archaic narcissistic configurations both within the transference and as they pervaded her life was seen most clearly in the change in her attitude in writing the dissertation. Jane identified with the analyst and gradually internalized the process of analysis as a model for work. The validation and evaluation of experience which had been the prerogative of idealized selfobjects gradually became a more autonomous function. She could begin to reject and accept ideas even though the elimination of an idea evoked anxiety. Her fears of suffering another narcissistic humiliation gradually lessened, so that work took on the usual rewarding and frustrating features.

In Jane's case the idealizations of others, the devaluations of herself, and the repressed grandiosity were
remnants of an arrest in development in which archaic
narcissistic configurations failed to become transformed
and internalized. The ballet incident and its consequences solidified the feeling of inadequacy while maintaining the grandiose self, in its archaic form, intact and
repressed. The symbioticlike attachment to and idealizations of her mother had gained additional strength
from the rebuff by her father and his empathic failure.
In turn, this placed further barriers in the path of Jane's
developing autonomy, self-assertion, and separation from
her mother. The vicissitudes of her grandiose self, her
idealizations of her mother and her surrogates, and the
symbioticlike attachment to them—all observable in
Jane's life from early childhood on—suggested that developmental arrests in the process of self-object separation contributed a major share in the genesis of her
psychopathology. The inability to perceive the real aspects of herself and others may thus be viewed as an
arrest at a prestage of defense, a by-product of specific
developmental failures. The process of treatment, while
reviving the significant object relations of her past in the
transference, also brought into sharp focus the extent to
which selfobjects were used to substitute for missing
psychic structure—specifically in the area of self-esteem
regulation.

IDEALIZATIONS AND GRANDIOSITY BASED
ON INTRAPSYCHIC CONFLICT

When Reginald began his analysis he was 22 years old,
single, and had graduated from college six months earlier. He did not have a job, nor had he sought one since
graduating. Working for a living was not a necessity for

him, since he, like Jane, was adequately supported by a trust fund set up by his parents. He had numerous acquaintances and a roommate, but no close male or female friends. He complained of feeling lonely, adrift, aimless, and directionless. Nothing seemed worthwhile or meaningful to him. Nothing—no activity, no job possibility, no female acquaintance—could evoke enthusiasm or excitement in him, and this made him feel disturbingly empty and hollow inside. He expressed reluctance to commit himself to any pursuit or person on the grounds that such a commitment entailed giving up all other possibilities. Yet he felt discontented with the tedium of his isolated, detached, and routinized existence.

Reginald was the youngest son in a wealthy, aristocratic New England family. His father, ten years older than his mother, was already in his late fifties when the patient was born. Reginald described him as "formal" and "fragile" and feared that any affectively charged situation "might break" him. His mother he described as "vivacious," "infantilizing," "domineering," and "castrating." "She was always on my back. . . . Everything had to be her way. . . . I was beaten down verbally. She could be incredibly sneaky and vicious, knows how to get you in your soft spots." She was "indestructible," the "control tower" of the family, either overwhelming the patient with verbal torrents or manipulating him by being easily hurt and playing the wounded martyr in the face of any opposition to her wishes. While his brother, four years older, was closer to his father, Reginald was more tied to his mother. In the course of his analysis he recovered childhood impressions that his mother used him as though he were an extension of her. Specifically, he became aware of feeling that she required his accomplishments to provide her the glory she sought and the penis she missed. When he began treatment, the patient still maintained a thinly disguised dependent attachment to her.

Reginald described his parents as continually relating to each other in "stylized formalities," which seemed to him like a foreign language from which he was excluded and which aroused his envy. His father invariably sought to keep the mother pacified by meeting her insatiable demands and soothing her easily hurt pride, while enjoining the patient to do the same. Hence, the parents presented a "united front," and his father provided no help to the patient in dealing with his mother. Reginald did find an ally in his brother, whom he admired because of his ability to deal aggressively with their mother through caustic humor. When his brother left for boarding school, Reginald felt terribly alone and overwhelmed by having to face his parents without his ally.

In the early analytic sessions the patient discussed his shame at still being a "virgin" and his fear of entering a sexual situation with a woman lest he expose his lack of knowledge of sexual matters and appear "incompetent, clumsy, and silly" in the woman's eyes. He avoided sexual experiences, anticipating a humiliating confrontation because of the gap between his fantasies of perfection and his actual "inexperience." He also feared the consequences of becoming immersed in feelings of intense sexual excitement. Such immersion would entail a dangerous relinquishing of control and render him helpless and vulnerable in relation to his partner, who, in his fantasies, took on the qualities of the vicious, domineering, castrating mother. Exploration of these fears enabled him to enter several tentative, mildly satisfying, but short-lived sexual involvements, which in turn paved the way for an investigation of his object relations. He inevitably sought women who were strong, aggressive, and "difficult," and his interest was not primarily in finding sexual satisfaction but rather in achieving a triumphant conquest by winning the woman's respect. His aim was not so much to use these women to enhance his self-esteem as to reverse the old defeat at the hands of his mother by triumphing over them. Having got the upper hand, Reginald would become fearful of being swallowed up by the woman's demands, as he had experienced with his mother, and would terminate the relationship.

Regarding his male acquaintances, it became clear that Reginald sought out men he perceived as superhuman, in possession of incredible strengths and intelligence, qualities he hoped to acquire by imitation. Gradually he revealed his need for an idealized analyst whose omnipotence and omniscience he could borrow and incorporate. In relation to the analyst Reginald was at first distrustful, guarded, controlled, and compliant. Above all, he wished to preserve harmony with the analyst in order to insure against any friction. He expressed an impelling need to experience the analyst as perfectly in tune with his emotions and wishes lest a breach in unity evoke dangerous feelings of frustration and hostility.

The patient's dreams began to reveal his rage both at his parents and at parent surrogates, most notably the analyst. The dangers of asserting oppositional and angry feelings were explored within the transference. The patient alternated between fear on the one hand that the analyst would paralyze him (as had his mother) with overwhelming verbal onslaughts and, on the other, that the analyst would respond with hurt martyrdom (again as had his mother) or would crumble and break in the face of his aggression (as he had imagined his father might). Furthermore, Reginald was in terror of the disruptive, disorganizing quality of his intense rage. His compromise solution in the face of these anxieties was to enact his hostility through passive resistance, with-holding, spiteful withdrawal, and detachment.

Along with the affects of anger and rage, Icarian themes began to appear in the patient's dreams: images of rising to great heights and plummeting to disaster. The imagery coincided with the unveiling of Reginald's grandiose self. He revealed his secret conviction that he possessed some special talent that had not yet blossomed but the existence of which he never doubted. He envis-aged that he would become a creative writer or painter, although his actual accomplishments in these areas were negligible. He believed that he possessed an extraordi-nary imagination, and was fascinated and amazed by the workings of his mind. He derived immense enjoyment from the random trains of verbal associations and images that paraded before his mind's eye during his many idle hours. Indeed, he was infatuated with an inflated image of himself as an imaginative genius. Further, he felt that his extraordinary imagination elevated him above the common folk, of whom he was contemptuous, and entitled him to special privileges and exemptions: his specialness entitled him to magic success and satisfaction and to exemption from the necessities of sustained effort and committed struggle. He was above the rules by which others have to play. In short, his grandiose self-image served to justify his "splendid isolation" and detachment.

Toward the end of the second year of treatment the patient had a spontaneous, "incidental" insight which illuminated the function of his self-aggrandizement and object-devaluation. He noticed that whenever he saw an attractive woman on the street he immediately devalued her in his mind and found reasons why she was not good enough for him. He suddenly realized that by so elevating himself and diminishing the woman he was protecting himself against feeling an intense longing for her as a highly idealized figure who, in turn, would evoke feelings of frustration and rage.

Shortly thereafter, the function of his grandiosity within the analytic transference was clarified. The patient phoned one evening and informed the analyst that he would miss his session the following morning and asked if he would have to pay for it. The analyst reminded him of the policy, to which the patient had agreed, that he would be charged for missed sessions unless sufficient notice were given. When Reginald appeared for his next session he coolly expressed his "annoyance" at having to submit to the rule. Although a recent dream had clearly indicated his growing dependence on an idealized image of the analyst as a kind of "guardian angel," he now felt that he should not have to pay at all for his analysis, since he viewed the analyst more as a "friend" than as a doctor. Analysis was "fun" and "enjoyable," but he did not really need the analyst's help. Next the patient produced the following dream:

> I could fly. I was flying around inside a beach club, near the ceiling. I was the only one who could fly. Everyone else was on the ground. Then I was swimming in a swimming pool. I realized I didn't have any bathing suit on. At first I was embarrassed. I didn't think not wearing a bathing suit was wrong, but I thought others would think it was wrong, and so I was uneasy. Then I lost my power to fly and was on the ground. Then I meditated for a while and concentrated on being able to fly again, and I could fly again. I enjoyed the flying and especially feeling that other people were envious of me. There was another part of the dream, very vague. Something about being down on the beach, at the ocean, and a big storm coming in.

Associations to successive elements in the dream emphasized his feeling of being independent and not bound by the rules and conventions that govern ordinary people, since his imaginative capacities put him above others.

This insistence on his overvaluation of his mental powers led to his hatred of being brought down to the ground by having to submit to the expectation that he pay for missed sessions like any other patient. Such a necessity challenged his grandiose self-elevation. Toward the end of the session he was able to link his erupting rage, of which he was becoming aware, with the dream image of the big storm coming in.

Analysis of the storm image led, in the course of several sessions, to a further understanding of the function of Reginald's grandiose self-image and his impelling need to sustain it. The storm represented the danger he would face in coming down from his lofty height and involving himself with others on the ground—the danger of stormy and disruptive affects associated with the resurgence of intrapsychic conflicts. With regard to the analyst, if the patient were to view him as a doctor whom he needed rather than as an envious, admiring friend, he would have to face his dependent longings and the analyst's failure to fulfill them, as well as his hurt, rage, and envy of the analyst. As described earlier, the emergence of aggressive affects and wishes raised the specter of highly dreaded danger situations associated with imagoes of the "overpowering" and "martyred" mother and the "crumbling" father. Thus, Reginald protected both himself and the object by "flying above" the analyst and the impending affective storms.

In Reginald's case there was little evidence that idealizations and grandiosity were rooted in structural deficiency or an arrest in representational development. In contrast to Jane, he did not reveal a history of severe narcissistic decompensations. Nor did he show any marked tendency toward self-object dedifferentiation in the analytic situation, despite the occurrence of transference "storms." His grandiosity was retained primarily to ward off perceptions of real aspects of the self which would have evoked dangerous affects (dependent longings, envy, rage) associated with intrapsychic conflicts and dreaded imagoes. Hence, in this case the classical technique of confronting, clarifying, and interpreting the defensive function of the patient's grandiosity and idealizations within the analytic transference was sufficient to elicit further meaningful associations and to promote therapeutic movement.

DISCUSSION

To highlight the differences between Jane and Reginald with respect to the roles that idealizations and grandiosity play for each, their apparent similarities will be considered first. From a descriptive, diagnostic standpoint, both patients would qualify for inclusion in either Kernberg's (1975) or Kohut's (1971) conceptualization of narcissistic personality disorder.

Conforming to Kernberg's description, both patients presented "a great need to be loved and admired . . . a very inflated concept of themselves and an inordinate need for tribute from others. . . . They envy others [and] tend to idealize some people from whom they expect narcissistic supplies. . . ." (pp. 227-228). For Kohut the crucial diagnostic criterion is the spontaneous development of a narcissistic transference in which the analyst serves as an idealized selfobject or as a mirror for the patient's own grandiose self. Jane and Reginald both established narcissistic transferences with idealizing and mirroring components for prolonged periods in their treatment.

Both patients exhibited a pronounced vulnerability in their self-esteem. In turn, relationships with people were burdened by an ever-present fear of rejection or humiliation. While Jane romanticized friends and analyst alike, endowing them with an aura of perfection, Reginald alternately idealized and devalued both his acquaintances and his analyst. For both, the real qualities of objects were thus obscured behind idealizations and devaluations, just as the real qualities of the self were obscured behind an archaic, grandiose self-image. For both, the inflated self-expectations—with respect to work, for example—precluded a realistic perception and utilization of abilities. On a more superficial level, both patients came from affluent backgrounds, had trust funds to support them, and had demonstrable pathology in their relation to work. Both complained of the meaninglessness of work and were convinced of the necessity of "keeping one's options open." For Reginald, the fear of a confrontation between the grandiose self and the actual self operated primarily in the area of his sexual life. His avoidance of sexual relationships was understood as stemming from a need to protect his grandiose expectations of sexual prowess from confrontation with a feared defective performance. Jane, too, protected her grandiose self by avoiding her dissertation, thereby averting a comparison between her expectation of writing "The Great American Dissertation" and her feared defective product.

The similarity in family constellation is also striking. Both patients sustained an attachment to an "intrusive" mother and recalled a "distant" relationship with the father. There is, of course, an obvious difference between the two patients—their sex. However, it seems to us that this difference per se was not decisive in promoting their respective psychopathologies.

We suggest that the decisive differences between these two patients with respect to their narcissistic pathology are found in the role of aggression and in the degree of intrapsychic separation from the mother (see Mahler et al., 1975). Both patients described their mothers as "intrusive," obstructing separation. For Reginald, however, his mother evoked considerable reactive aggression which, for better or worse, fostered separation. Her intrusiveness carried with it a castrative threat, and he responded with a spiteful withdrawal. He defensively retreated into his "splendid isolation" and revengeful fantasies of triumph over her. The fact that his mother became a castrative threat insured her position as a more or less separate object rather than as a selfobject; i.e., she was not retained as a source of self-esteem regulation. Hence he achieved a degree of separation from her, although at the price of perpetuating severe conflicts over aggression as well as the pathological narcissism that evolved to defend against them, as exemplified in his dream and the transference crisis to which it referred. Jane's mother, though obstructing the process of establishing self-object boundaries, never became so great a threat and did not evoke overwhelming anger. Jane's mother remained idealized and a source of narcissistic sustenance. As shown in Jane's religious period, her expressions of and defenses against aggression paled in the face of her need to maintain her mother as an idealized selfobject, a need to which her later narcissistic pathology became heir. At those rare times when Jane did oppose her mother and her surrogates, it was in a context that never threatened the symbioticlike attachments.

As a consequence of these developmental differences, dependency feelings played a different role for each. Reginald defended himself against experiencing the vulnerability of his self-esteem, while Jane both accepted and despised the vulnerability as a syntonic aspect of her self representation. Jane devalued herself for her dependence on others, whereas Reginald devalued others in his attempt to deny his dependence on them and his vulnerability to their reactions.

Differences could be noticed in the degree of conscious awareness of the grandiose self and the idealizations of others. Jane repressed the grandiose self (though it was implicit in "The Great American Dissertation"), and its uncovering in the analysis evoked shame. Reginald consciously kept the grandiose self secret, and its uncovering in his confrontation with the rules of payment in analysis evoked anxiety, rage, and an exacerbation of his imperiousness. Behind his grandiosity was his envy and rage, rooted in his exclusion from his parents' united front. Jane's grandiosity reflected a reemergence of phase-appropriate exhibitionism, prematurely repressed.

Jane's idealizations of her friends were conscious and, to her, justified. Their deidealization within the analysis was a gradual process. Certain of Reginald's idealizations were uncovered through the analysis of his fantasies when he saw attractive women. These idealizations had been repressed lest awareness of them confront him with the enormity of his need for these women and his fear of falling embarrassingly short of their "inordinate" expectations.

While Jane's grandiosity was a remnant of an arrested development in which her self-esteem had been traumatically deflated, Reginald's grandiosity was defensive in nature. It served to deny his vulnerability and his realistic limitations. Furthermore, it shielded him from the intrusions and "onslaughts" of his mother and her surrogates and from his own highly conflictual reactive aggression. For Jane the idealization of others was a perpetuation of the idealization of her mother as a selfobject, and actual contact had to be maintained with them to prevent fragmentation of her self representation. The presence of these idealizations thus signaled a specific failure in separation and internalization. For Reginald the idealizations of others were an expression of a conflictual need for them and warded off rage and envy toward others as replicas of the castrative mother.

We are suggesting that two apparently similar narcissistic personality patterns can be arrived at by different ontogenetic pathways. We believe that this justifies the postulation of two types of narcissistic disorder requiring different treatment approaches: narcissistic pathology which is the remnant of a developmental arrest at a prestage of defense and narcissistic pathology resulting from defenses against intrapsychic conflicts. We are also suggesting that the role of aggression differs in the two types. In the subgroup of patients (like Jane and the patients described by Kohut) for whom narcissistic pathology is the remnant of a developmental arrest, aggressive affects and wishes were never sufficient to counter their symbioticlike involvements. The mergerlike attachments of these patients were more sustaining than they were threatening to their autonomy. Their anxiety was aroused when they were threatened with phase-appropriate separation.

Patients in both subgroups have suffered traumatic disappointments in their narcissistic attachments. However, in the subgroup of patients (like Reginald and the patients described by Kernberg) for whom narcissistic pathology is defensive, rage plays a more pronounced role. They seek safety not in merger but in flight and isolation. Self-object boundaries are not obliterated but defensively fortified. Their anxiety stems from a fear that their defenses against their need for others will be ruptured.

In narcissistic pathology rooted in a developmental arrest, idealizations and grandiosity reflect a failure to attain adequate self-object differentiation and an inability to register and affirm the real qualities of the self and objects (arrest at a prestage of defense). In defensive nar-

cissistic pathology, idealizations and grandiosity serve
to deny real qualities of the self and objects which could
be perceived but which are associated with intrapsychic
conflicts.

There is no evidence to indicate that the formation of
defensive narcissistic pathology is necessarily preceded
by a phase during which arrested developmental aspects
predominate. Our observations are that the genetic and
functional explanations of Kernberg (1975) and Kohut
(1971) have validity for different patients and for different phases of treatment. The analytic approaches which
grow out of these divergent formulations address themselves to predominantly different areas of pathology.

Kohut's treatment approach aims at permitting the
arrested narcissistic configurations to unfold as they
would have had the process not been prematurely, traumatically interrupted. In turn, these archaic configurations can be transformed into more mature forms of self-
esteem regulation. Kernberg's treatment approach aims
at exposing the defenses against dependency, rage, and
envy, specifically in the transference. In turn, with an
acceptance of the need for others, guilt for hurting them
and gratitude for what is received from them can develop.
The character traits of haughty isolation, contempt, and
grandiosity become unnecessary, and aggression can become better integrated and contribute to mature object
love (Kernberg, 1976).

SUMMARY

We have distinguished idealizations and grandiosity
based on a developmental inability to register and affirm
the real qualities of the self and objects (prestage of defense) from idealizations and grandiosity in which there
is a defensive denial of the real qualities of the self and

objects. We described two cases of narcissistic disturbance which illustrate the proposed distinction. We suggest that apparently similar narcissistic personality patterns can be arrived at by divergent ontogenetic pathways, with crucial differences in the role of aggression and the degree of self-object separation attained. Hence, we postulate two types of narcissistic disorder: narcissistic pathology which is the remnant of a developmental arrest, and narcissistic pathology resulting from defenses against intrapsychic conflicts. We contend that Kohut's formulations and treatment recommendations have validity for the former, whereas Kernberg's approach is applicable to the latter.

6

Projection, Incorporation, and Splitting

Our aim here is to amplify our proposal that there is a developmental line for each defensive process, with pre-stages of the defenses occurring prior to the consolidation of self and object representations.

The extension of psychoanalytic practice beyond the classical neuroses to severe narcissistic, borderline, and psychotic conditions has made it necessary to distinguish between psychopathology which results from structural conflict and psychopathology which is rooted in an arrest in representational development. Structural conflict can only come about after certain prerequisite internalizations have occurred, when self-object differentiation and representational integration are well under way and preoedipal configurations are regressively revived in the service of defense. For ego and superego functions to participate in intrapsychic conflict, considerable structuralization of self and object representations must have occurred (Arlow, 1963).

Whereas the term structural conflict is generally applied to vicissitudes of sexual and aggressive wishes toward objects, developmental arrest is the term usually applied to failures in the development of ego and superego functions and in particular to interferences with specific aspects of self-object differentiation and representational integration. The diagnostic significance of this distinction was alluded to by Freud (1911a) and Ferenczi (1913) even before the creation of the structural theory (see also A. Freud, 1965; Zetzel, 1966). A developmental arrest can come about through an unfavorable match between the environment and the developing child, either because the child's unfolding potentialities are not met by an average expectable environment or because the child's needs require a particular empathic responsiveness which the environment fails to provide. Consequently, certain internalizations crucial for the structuralization of the representational world are interfered with.

An examination of the history of the concept of defense indicates that while ideas about *what* a defense wards off have evolved, the concept of defense itself has remained static. Before Hartmann's studies of ego functions, only instincts were seen to develop autonomously. Thus a defense was viewed as a mental operation called into service by a phase-specific psychosexual threat. The study of psychosexual development was therefore an appropriate means for understanding conflict, particularly its defensive aspects. After Hartmann's (1939) elaboration of the concept of an undifferentiated id-ego matrix out of which ego functions become differentiated and unfold, some ego functions gained autonomy; the defenses, however, remained wedded to and dependent upon psychosexual development. Several writers (e.g., A. Freud, 1936; Jacobson, 1971, ch. 4; Gedo and Goldberg, 1973; Kernberg, 1976, ch. 1) have attempted to introduce a temporal scheme by ranking defenses from "archaic" (denial and splitting) to "higher order" (repression). Anna Freud (1936), however, cautioning against the attempt at chronological classification of defenses, stated: "It will probably be best to abandon the attempt so to classify them and, instead, to study in detail the situations which call forth the defensive reactions" (p. 53).

Matching specific defenses with substages of psychosexual development is a relic of Abraham's ontogenetic table (see Fliess, 1948). This approach presupposes a high correlation between psychosexual development and the maturation of ego functions. However, as Ross (1970) and Lachmann (1975) have pointed out, this correlation has been greatly overestimated, and clinical experience has offered much contradictory data. By keeping the concept of defense so closely tied to psychosexual development and, hence, to infantile conflict, analysts have failed to give sufficient attention to defense in the context of an evolving representational world. Advances in the understanding of representational development and the pathology of self and object representations have therefore failed to contribute to the understanding of defensive processes. We believe we are now in a better position to examine defenses, not only as they ward off sexual and aggressive wishes, but also in relation to the development of self and object representations. We recognize that a defense is a complex psychological function which requires a particular level of representational differentiation and integration before it can be called into service.

Our work has led us to propose that there is a developmental line for each defensive process and that a defense in the usual sense of the term represents the endpoint of a series of developmental achievements (for a different approach to this issue, see Spitz [1961] and Gedo and Goldberg [1973]). Hence, the utilization of a particular defense not only has relevance for understanding a specific intrapsychic conflict, but indicates as well that certain prerequisite developmental tasks have been accomplished.

In the two preceding chapters, we described the circumstances under which pathological idealizations, grandiosity, and other failures to perceive and acknowledge reality accurately reflect a developmental arrest at prestages of defense, and described as well the circumstances under which they result from defensive processes (such as denial) as part of a structural conflict. We tried to bridge these two explanatory models and discussed the relevant differences between them. In the present chapter we extend this examination of developmental prestages to certain other defenses which, like denial, idealization, and grandiosity, radically alter the perception of the self and of the object world. The mental operations to be considered are projection, incorporation, and splitting. Specific reference will be made to their *defensive* use, in which they ward off components of a structural conflict, and to the occurrence of their *prestages* as an aspect of an arrest in development.

DEFENSES AND THEIR
DEVELOPMENTAL PRESTAGES

Our study of denial served as a prototype for understanding the ontogenesis of a defense. Having extended this developmental framework to a consideration of idealizations and grandiosity, we now apply it to some additional defenses which operate primarily through the distortion of self and object representations: projection, incorporation, and splitting. We have chosen to focus on this group of defenses because recent advances in psychoanalytic developmental psychology are especially germane to the elucidation of the developmental prestages of those defenses which operate by altering aspects of the representational world.

Projection as a defense may be viewed as a process

whereby painful affects or ideas originating in the self representation are experienced as originating in one or more object representations in order to alleviate intrapsychic structural conflict (Freud, 1911b, 1922; Waelder, 1951). We are defining incorporation here as a complementary process whereby portions of an object representation are relocated in the self representation. As a defense, incorporation typically functions to ward off intrapsychic conflicts in the context of disappointment by, separation from, or loss of, an ambivalently loved object (Freud, 1915a). Projections and incorporations, in our view, are basically fantasy formations, analogous to denial fantasies, which attempt to eliminate from awareness aspects of the representational world associated with painful affects and intrapsychic conflict.

The developmental prestages of projection and incorporation can be found in the normal symbiotic states of earliest infancy, in which self and object representations are undifferentiated, and in the somewhat later infantile states of partial self-object differentiation and partial self-object boundary confusion (cf., Jacobson, 1964; Spitz, 1966; Mahler et al., 1975). An example of the latter would be toddlers who believe their mothers know their thoughts or have put thoughts into their heads, the normal developmental equivalent of the psychotic "influencing machine" (Tausk, 1919). Indeed, some analysts who have worked with psychotic patients have alluded to or specifically noted the crucial role of arrests in development at, or regressions to, levels of incomplete self-object differentiation and inadequate self-object boundary maintenance (Ferenczi, 1913; Tausk, 1919; Federn, 1927; Searles, 1959; Jacobson, 1971, ch. 10; Kohut, 1971; Kernberg, 1975).

It should be stressed that projection and incorporation as defenses actively employed to ward off structural conflict can come into play only after a minimum of self-object differentiation has been achieved (A. Freud, 1936; Gedo and Goldberg, 1973). Defensive translocation of mental content across self-object boundaries requires that those boundaries have in large part been consolidated. Clearly, one's therapeutic approach to states of self-object confusion will differ radically, depending upon whether they are regarded as stemming from defensive projections and incorporations which serve to ward off intrapsychic conflict, or as rooted in an arrest in development at or regression to an early prestage of these defenses characterized by an inability to adequately differentiate self and object images.

Kernberg's (1975) discussion of "projective identification," which he regards as a form of projection characteristic of borderline patients, fails to make these distinctions adequately. He writes (italics added):

> Patients with borderline personality organization tend to present very strong projective trends, but it is not only the quantitative predominance of projection but also the qualitative aspect of it which is characteristic. The *main purpose of projection here is to externalize the all-bad, aggressive self and object images,* and the main consequence of this need is the development of dangerous, retaliatory objects against which the patient has to defend himself. This projection of aggression is rather unsuccessful. While these patients do have sufficient development of ego boundaries to be able to differentiate self and objects in most areas of their lives, the very intensity of the projective needs, plus *the general ego weakness* characterizing these patients, *weakens ego boundaries* in the particular area of the projection of aggression. This leads such patients to feel that they can still identify themselves with the object onto whom aggression has been projected, and their ongoing "empathy" with the now threatening object maintains and increases the fear of their own projected aggression. . . . In summary, projective identification is characterized by the *lack of differentiation*

between self and object in that particular area, by *continuing to experience the impulse as well as the fear of that impulse while the projection is active,* and by the need to control the external object [pp. 30-31].

On the one hand, "projective identification" is described as a defensive operation actively employed to ward off conflictual aggressive affects and wishes. On the other, it is also seen to reflect "general ego weakness" and inadequate achievement of self-object differentiation (developmental arrest). We believe that at particular points in treatment a diagnostic judgment should be made on whether the self-object confusion in question results primarily from defensive activity or from an arrest at a prestage of defense. Ideally, one's technical approach will be strictly dictated by this assessment. We find it difficult to view "projective identification" primarily as a defense, since the conflictual affect or wish continues to be experienced consciously as an aspect of *both* self representation and object representation. Hence, we prefer to view "projective identification" primarily as a remnant or revival of an arrested prestage of defense and to gear our initial therapeutic approach to the developmental deficiency in self-object boundary maintenance.

An ambiguity similar to that found in Kernberg's discussion of projective identification appears in Jacobson's (1971, ch. 10) concept of "psychotic identifications." She explains them alternately as: (1) reflecting a "fixation"[1] at infantile states of magic participation, in which self and object images are incompletely differentiated—that

---

[1] In our opinion, the term fixation should be reserved for the vicissitudes of psychosexual development, and the term developmental arrest used to refer to interferences with self-object differentiation and representational integration.

is, a developmental arrest at a prestage of defense; (2) resulting from defensive incorporations which aim at safeguarding an object relationship by turning aggression away from the ambivalently loved object onto the self; and (3) stemming from a regressive flight from intrapsychic conflict to undifferentiated states—that is, a defensive regression to a prestage of incorporation. As we stated earlier, the use of incorporation as a defense requires that self-object boundaries have in large part been consolidated. In Jacobson's first explanation, self-object confusion reflects a developmental arrest at a prestage of defense, in the second it results from defensive incorporations, in the third it stems from defensive regression (revival of archaic states) but *not* from defensive incorporation. We find it difficult to accept that these three processes are compatible theoretically; further, we believe that each implies a different therapeutic approach.

Splitting as a defense may be viewed as a process whereby object images (and/or self images) with opposing affective colorations are forcibly dissociated or experientially kept apart in order to alleviate intense ambivalence conflicts (see Kernberg, 1975, 1976, ch. 1; Mahler et al., 1975). In our view, such split images are essentially fantasy formations which, like projections, incorporations, and denial fantasies, aim to distort aspects of the representational world that are linked to intrapsychic conflict. The normal prestages of splitting can be found in early infantile states in which the child is developmentally incapable of integrating object (and self) images with opposing affective colorations (Spitz, 1966; Zetzel, 1966; Atkin, 1975; Kernberg, 1975, 1976; Pruyser, 1975). As with projection and incorporation, it should be stressed that splitting as a defense actively employed to ward off intrapsychic conflict can come into play only after a minimum of integration of oppositely colored object (and self) images has been accomplished through development. A defensive split into parts requires a prior integration of a whole (Atkin, 1975; Pruyser, 1975). Again, one's therapeutic approach to unintegrated representations will depend upon whether they are regarded as resulting from defensive splitting or as reflecting an arrest in development at an early prestage of splitting characterized by an inability to integrate affectively contrasting images.

The distinction we are emphasizing was prefigured historically in early descriptions of hysterical patients, many of whom we would now regard as borderline personalities. Specifically, we are referring to the contrasting views of Janet and Freud with respect to hysterical "splitting of consciousness" (see Pruyser, 1975). Janet regarded hysterical dissociations as stemming from a constitutionally determined curtailment of "psychical synthesis," whereas Freud interpreted them as resulting from resistance—that is, repressions instituted in connection with intrapsychic conflict.

This same dichotomy now appears in current literature on the borderline personality. For instance, Atkin (1975) presents case material which he believes "offers strong evidence of the primary etiological importance of a constitutional defect in the integrative and synthetic functions in the formation of a borderline personality" (p. 31). Kernberg (1975), on the other hand, regards the "lack of synthesis of contradictory self and object images" in borderline personalities as evidence of an active defensive splitting process aimed at warding off severe ambivalence conflicts (p. 28).

With regard to the propositions of Janet and Atkin, we believe that the concept of an arrest in development (which Atkin himself uses) eliminates both the necessity and advisability of making any a priori assumptions about so-called constitutional defects in an effort to explain psychopathology that is not primarily grounded in intrapsychic conflict. Indeed, this nature-nurture antithesis may be viewed as a relic of the stage of psychoanalytic conceptualization that existed before it was recognized that ego functions develop autonomously. The development of self and object representations proceeds as a result of the complex interplay of constitutional and experiential factors, and in most cases the relative contribution of constitution and experience to a developmental arrest in the integrative function would be virtually impossible to ascertain. To invoke arbitrarily the concept of constitutional defect as an explanation introduces an unwarranted degree of therapeutic pessimism. What Atkin views as evidence for a constitutional defect in the integrative and synthetic functions, we would see as evidence of no more than an arrest in development at a prestage of defensive splitting.

Kernberg (1975) has cogently described the prestages of defensive splitting in early infantile states:

Introjections and identifications established under the influence of libidinal drive derivatives are at first built up separately from those established under the influence of aggressive drive derivatives ("good" and "bad" internal objects, or "positive" and "negative" introjections). This division of internalized object relations into "good" and "bad" happens at first simply because of the lack of integrative capacity of the early ego. Later on, what originally was a lack of integrative capacity is used defensively by the emerging ego in order to prevent the generalization of anxiety and to protect the ego core built around positive introjections. . . . *This defensive division of the ego, in which what was at first a simple defect in integration is then used actively for other purposes, is in essence the mechanism of splitting* [p. 25].

Curiously, despite this illuminating developmental formulation, Kernberg appears to assume that whenever

unintegrated representations appear in a borderline personality, they stem from defensive splitting, which "is
maintained as an essential mechanism preventing dif-
fusion of anxiety within the ego and protecting the positive introjections and identifications" (p. 28) against
invasion by aggressive affects. His treatment approach
follows directly from this assumption. We would stress,
however, that the need to protect an object relationship
from aggressive feelings and wishes presupposes a min-
imal integration of the object image. We do not believe
that such a presuppostion is warranted a priori in every
borderline case. As with states of self-object confusion,
in any given occurrence of unintegrated representations
a diagnostic judgment must be made about whether the
lack of integration of object and/or self images results
from defensive splitting or stems from a developmental
arrest at a prestage of this defense. One's technical approach will be determined accordingly. We suggest that
those instances in which contrasting "all-good" and "all-
bad" object images are rigidly linked to two or more separate external objects, as in split transferences, are likely
to stem from the operation of defensive splitting which
aims to ward off intense ambivalence conflicts. On the
other hand, the fluid and rapid alternation of contradictory images in connection with the same external object
is more likely to reflect an arrest in development at a
prestage of splitting characterized by an inability to integrate affectively contrasting representations.

CLINICAL ILLUSTRATIONS

In our work on idealization and grandiosity, we suggested
that Kohut's (1971) treatment recommendations (aimed
at permitting archaic narcissistic configurations to unfold and become subject to transformation into mature

forms of self-esteem regulation) are specifically valid for narcissistic pathology which is the remnant of a developmental arrest. By contrast, Kernberg's (1975) treatment recommendations (aimed at exposing narcissistic resistances) are applicable to narcissistic pathology resulting from defenses against intrapsychic conflicts. A schematic comparison of the two suggests that the essence of Kohut's technical suggestions is to focus empathically on the *state which the developmentally arrested patient needs to maintain or achieve,* whereas Kernberg strongly emphasizes interpreting *what the defending patient needs to ward off.*

As illustrated in the clinical vignettes to follow, we believe that these two treatment approaches offer, respectively, prototypes for treating clinical manifestations of developmental arrests at prestages of defense and for treating those aspects of the patient's psychopathology deriving from defenses against structural conflict. The role of genetic reconstructions will differ in the two treatment paradigms. In the case of pathology rooted in structural conflict, historical reconstructions alert the analyst to the infantile satisfactions and fantasies that the patient will *wish to repeat* in the transference. This wish to repeat and its attendant anxieties and defenses will then become the focus of analytic exploration. In the case of a developmental arrest, reconstructions of the patient's past alert the analyst to the pathogenic developmental traumata which the analyst will *strive not to repeat* with the patient. The patient's reactions to the inevitable unwitting repetitions which do occur then become a focus of analysis. With structural conflict, early experiences have been *repressed* or otherwise defended against. These are reanimated and analyzed in the transference. With a developmental arrest, experiences that the patient legitimately *needed but missed* or prematurely lost are understood within the transference in order to assist the patient in his belated development.

Defensive Projection and "Projective Identification"

When Bill, 25 and single, began his analysis, he was suffering from a severe narcissistic disturbance. During the early months of his treatment, especially when he discussed his difficulties in relating socially and sexually to women, he attributed to the analyst attitudes of extreme contempt, disgust, and devaluation, a process that frequently reached paranoid intensity. Interpretations to the effect that Bill was experiencing his own self-devaluations as coming from the person of the analyst were met at first with anxiety, anger, resistance, and an intensification of persecutory feelings in the transference. But these interpretations eventually enabled the patient to experience and explore his own attitudes of searing self-contempt and self-disgust. Here the patient's self-object confusion within the transference resulted from a defensive projection which aimed to substitute interpersonal for intrapsychic conflicts. Therapeutic movement was fostered by interpreting what was being warded off—Bill's merciless self-hatred.

By the third year of treatment Bill had established a narcissistic transference which oscillated between "merger," "twinship," and "mirror transference proper" (Kohut, 1971). The transference at this time reflected a therapeutic regression to an archaic prestage at which the patient's representational development had been arrested. During this period of the therapy, Bill was discussing certain of his sadistic sexual fantasies having to do with molesting and mutilating children. Suddenly he became panic stricken. He exclaimed that the analyst's accepting attitude must mean that the analyst had the same sadistic fantasies. Further, Bill imagined that he and his analyst could become involved in a collusive relationship in which they enacted those fantasies in reality. These thoughts were extremely frightening to the patient.

The state of self-object confusion described above would seem to fit Kernberg's (1975) description of "projective identification," which we have earlier discussed as a prestage of projection. Bill consciously experienced the sadistic fantasies as an aspect of both his self representation and his object representation of the analyst, because the distinction between self and object had been weakened by the revival of an archaic selfobject configuration.

Interpretations of this material in terms of defensive operations might have aimed at uncovering to what extent the fantasies of mutilating children represented an identification with the aggressor (parent) and to what extent the patient was attempting to ward off masochistic transference wishes by becoming preoccupied with the sadistic fantasies. Indeed, much later in the analysis, when sufficient structuralization of the patient's representational world was present, these defensive aspects of his fantasies became subject to systematic interpretation. At this earlier point in treatment, however, the analyst commented on Bill's need to have it demonstrated that while the analyst could accept his fantasies he did not entertain the same fantasies and would not tolerate their being enacted in reality. In contrast to what would be expected when confronting a defensive projection, this intervention, focusing on the patient's developmentally determined self-object confusion and his phase-appropriate need to achieve more adequate self-object differentiation, had the effect of relieving (rather than increasing) his anxiety. It did not evoke resistance, and it quickly

enabled Bill to continue to explore his own fantasies.
Therapeutic movement was fostered by empathically focusing on Bill's need to establish a firmer distinction
between his self representation as a person who could not
control sexual and aggressive urges and his object representation of the analyst as a person who could.

Defensive Incorporation and Its Prestages

There are many examples of defensive projection and
defensive incorporation in the analytic literature and in
analytic practice. Bill's defensive projection of his self-
devaluation onto the analyst served to ward off painful
feelings of self-hatred. In the case of Anna, whose treatment was described in chapter 4, her fully conscious conviction that a small penis protruded from between her
vaginal lips illustrates clearly the operation of defensive
incorporation.

It was possible to reconstruct that the rudiments of
Anna's penis fantasy appeared as a direct response to her
father's imprisonment and eventual death in a concentration camp when she was four years old. Two complementary explanations for the illusory penis emerged.
According to the first, she imagined that her father had
disappeared and stayed away because she was disgusting
and valueless to him: her genital was defective, damaged,
and "castrated"; she had no penis. She developed the fantasy of possessing a penis, then, in order to repair her
"defect," as an expression of her wish to make her father
value her and return to her now that she was "whole."
According to the second explanation, the fantasy was an
attempt to restore her father to her through incorporation, to rescue and enshrine a part of him in her own
body image. The illusory penis made up for the loss of
the whole object by incorporating a highly valued part-
object.

At some point during her latency years, when she had become able to comprehend the reality of her father's death, Anna began to construct an elaborate denial-in-fantasy system by which she kept her father alive and prevented a developmentally possible mourning process. The illusory penis functioned as a central ingredient in her denial system. It sustained her conviction that her father was alive and that he stayed away because she was genitally defective and disgusting to him. At this point the illusory penis may be described as a defensive incorporation and denial fantasy which warded off the intense ambivalence conflicts evoked by Anna's growing comprehension of her father's death. She needed to preserve the hope that he would return to shelter and love her; she also felt terribly guilty and magically blamed herself for his death.

In Anna's analysis, there was no evidence of arrests in the structuralization of her representational world. Hence, we must assume that her relatively benign preoedipal years had provided her with differentiated self and object representations and stable self-object boundaries by the time of her father's death. The illusory penis was regarded as a defensive incorporation of the paternal phallus, and the various intrapsychic conflicts that it served to ward off in the course of Anna's development became the focus of systematic interpretation. Analysis of the functions of the penis fantasy was met with anxiety, resistance, and rage-filled struggles with the analyst. However, when the multiple dangers that it warded off were sufficiently explored and understood (especially within the transference), the illusory penis and associated feelings of defectiveness were completely dissolved.

In the case of Jane, whose treatment we described in chapter 5, states of self-object confusion occurred as the halo of idealized objects fell upon her self. Whereas in Bill's sadistic fantasies the self-object confusion reflected a prestage of projection, in Jane's case it may be described as a prestage of incorporation.

Analysis of Jane's attachment to a group of idealized friends led to an elucidation of the specific vulnerability in her self-esteem. She experienced these friends as concrete embodiments of her parents' ideals and, hence, of her own self-expectations. Proximity to them enhanced her self representation by making her feel worthy and acceptable—her "gilt by association."

The extent to which her self-esteem varied according to her distance from these idealized objects, and with every nuance of their reactions to her, indicated the extent to which self and object images were insufficiently distinguished from each other. A smile or a frown from the object immediately resulted in either a positively or negatively toned self-perception. Although Jane's self-esteem rose in consequence of favorable contact with her friends, the value that she "borrowed" remained the property of the object and was perceived as part of the self only so long as actual contact was maintained.

With Anna, the defensive incorporation of the paternal phallus occurred in the context of very specific intrapsychic conflicts and warded off equally specific dangers associated with particular objects. In contrast, Jane's frequent manifestations of self-object confusion were neither conflict-specific nor object-specific. They occurred in a wide variety of interpersonal relationships that were used for self-esteem regulation because her self representation was insufficiently structuralized. Jane's strivings for self-esteem through states of symbioticlike merger with idealized objects are best conceptualized as reflecting a developmental arrest at a prestructural prestage of incorporation.

The therapeutic approach to Anna's illusory penis was to systematically analyze its defensive functions. To have interpreted strictly in defensive terms Jane's attempts to acquire the valued aspects of her friends through literal closeness to them would have placed her in an untenable position. She would have felt pressure to dispense with an essential ingredient needed to sustain her precarious and vulnerable self representation. In submission to the analyst she might have expressed greater self-assertion with her friends or voiced resentment or envy of them, but in consequence of the self-object confusion she would have paid a high price in lowered self-esteem. The analyst first had to help Jane gradually define self-object boundaries by conveying an understanding of the narcissistic function of the bond she was trying to maintain with both her friends and her analyst, and by responding appropriately when the symbioticlike transference had outlived its usefulness and steps toward greater separation were becoming possible. Empathic clarifications of the purpose of her merger experiences and, later, of her readiness to accept separateness evoked neither anxiety nor resistance. Instead, Jane appreciated and used such interventions to facilitate increasingly autonomous efforts at self-articulation.

Defensive Splitting and Its Prestages

Rachel employed defensive splitting in the context of very specific intrapsychic conflicts in relation to particular object images. When she began treatment at the age of 27, she suffered from a morbid dread of becoming trapped in elevators, as well as from wrenching ambivalence conflicts in her relationships with men. Her mother, with whom she had maintained a very close tie, had slowly deteriorated and died of cancer when Rachel was fifteen. Her father had died a year and a half later, following a period of prolonged psychological deterioration in consequence of his wife's death.

During the fourth year of her analysis, Rachel presented a highly illuminating dream, fragments of which are germane to the subject of splitting:

> I was living in a hotel, a resort in the countryside, with Bernard [her 60-year-old lover]. It was really strange because there were two Bernards—a Bernard and another Bernard who was dying. He was lying in bed and dying. I was taking care of him and figured that since he was dying, I'd make him die faster. So I got some arsenic and mixed it with the medicine I was giving him and he died. . . . Something about the resort reminded me of places I went with my parents as a child. I explained to Bernard that I'd killed Bernard because, since he was dying anyway, I wanted to experiment with killing.

In association to the theme of the two Bernards, Rachel recounted that when she and Bernard were doing things together, he seemed like a very vigorous and glamorous figure, and she loved to be with him. However, she recalled that on certain occasions when she saw him lying in bed asleep, he appeared to her to be very old and decrepit, and she felt totally disgusted and repelled by him. Bringing the discrepant images of Bernard into juxtaposition evoked an acute conflict of ambivalence: "One side of me recognizes he's too old for me, and the other side wants to stick with him. When I see how old he is, I want to kill him so I can turn to younger men."

Rachel then became tearful as she began to confront the reality that Bernard would certainly die while she was still a young woman and she would have to suffer "the terrible pain of separation." She wept as she spoke of her experiences at her mother's bedside and her revulsion at the intolerable sight of her mother's helplessness and deterioration (feelings she experienced again in reaction to her father's psychological deterioration). The analyst interpreted that the patient needed to keep separate her images of Bernard as vigorous and glamorous (her perception of him when he was awake) and as aging (her perception of him when he slept) lest bringing them together would revive her conflicting feelings in the presence of her dying mother. Rachel then remembered her tormenting wishes to speed up her mother's death in order to be free of her, along with her oppressive fears of dire punishment for her guilty wishes.

In Rachel's analysis there was no evidence of a developmental arrest in the integrative function. She was quite capable (structurally) of experiencing contradictory affects in relation to a whole, ambivalently loved object, as evidenced in her relations with younger men (including her analyst) who did *not* reanimate the particular image of a dying parent. The unintegrated images of Bernard had resulted from defensive splitting, and the analyst was able, through interpretation, to promote the uncovering of the specific ambivalence conflict that was being warded off.

Rachel showed no evidence of borderline psychopathology in spite of her use of splitting, often considered pathognomonic of such pathology. It is precisely with the borderline patient that a diagnostic distinction between the defense and its prestages is most germane. The prestages of defensive splitting have been described in terms of an arrest in the ability to synthesize or integrate divergent perceptions of an object (or the self). Developmentally, this would hark back to the period in infancy when alternating affective states completely determine the infant's perceptions of objects. This occurs prior to the establishment of object constancy and, when maintained into adulthood, indicates serious interferences with aspects of reality perception. Clinical examples of the prestages of splitting would thus be more characteristically found in the more severely disturbed borderline, prepsychotic and psychotic patients.

The case presented by Atkin (1975) of a 36-year-old

woman with borderline pathology exemplifies both the
use of splitting for defensive purposes and the occurrence
of prestages of that defense. Atkin describes in detail this
woman's "integrative 'disjunction' manifested by simul-
taneous but nonconflictual strivings toward contradictory goals" (p. 29). The patient voiced glaringly
contradictory expectations and discrepant evaluations of
the same person within one analytic session. Unlike
Rachel's use of splitting, this failure to integrate psychic
contents did not appear to be linked to specific intrapsychic conflicts. Rather, her integrative incapacity pervaded broad areas of her cognitive and conative functioning
so that she lived in an experiential world of unsynthe-
sized "part-universes" and "need-satisfying part-objects."

Within the framework of our proposed distinction between prestages of splitting and its function as a defense,
we would agree with Atkin's demonstration that there
had been a developmental arrest in the synthetic or integrative function. Hence, in the early phase of treatment, confronting the patient with her inconsistencies
evoked neither anxiety nor resistance, but rather non-
comprehension. In this phase, according to Atkin, the
analyst unwittingly served as a "pregenital parent," offering his own unified perceptions as models for internalization, which assisted the patient in the task of
integration. During a later phase of therapy, when sufficient structuralization had been accomplished, the patient used disjunctive phenomena defensively, and their
analysis evoked anxiety and resistance.

We must, of course, recognize that such a division of
the course of treatment into "prestructural" and "defensive" phases is schematic and oversimplified. Even in the
early period of the therapy, Atkin's patient showed some
evidence of defensive splitting in the transference. The
analyst was maintained as an idealized all-good object,

while the patient's parents were hated and experienced
as all-bad. Here splitting was used defensively to safe-
guard the image of the analyst by warding off and dis-
placing the patient's aggressive wishes toward him. In
the prestage of splitting, as exemplified in the alternating contradictory attitudes toward the same object, no
conflictual wishes seemed to be warded off; rather, a developmental inability to integrate discrepant psychic
contents was in evidence. In the defensive splitting of the
transference, representations of the self, the analyst, and
the parents were more clearly articulated, so that hostile
wishes reserved for the parents could be excluded from
the relationship with the analyst.

The prestage of splitting in which the same object is
alternately seen as comforting and as dangerous—reflective of a developmental arrest in the capacity to synthesize aspects of self and object representations—was
also seen in the case of Burton, a patient being seen by
a therapist under the supervision of one of the authors.
Burton began his fifth attempt at psychotherapeutic
treatment at age twenty, with a history of persecutory
delusions, alternating acute suicidal and homicidal
preoccupations, and fears of "imminent disintegration."
In the early months of treatment there were session-to-
session oscillations from intense distrust and fear of being
influenced against his will and even annihilated by the
therapist, to feeling understood and wishing to merge
with her. His view of the therapist alternated between
seeing her as murderous and depriving or as all-good and
giving. These perceptions were associated with recollections of gross inconsistencies in his mother's behavior
toward him: he remembered her as overtly sexually seductive and as having subjected him to severe daily beatings from the time he was two years old.

Burton's earliest memories were of these daily beatings and of lying in his crib in the morning, waiting for his father to smack him for crying so early in the day. By the age of three or four, he began to have repetitive nightmares, one of a tick-tock noise which eventually exploded into an atomic bomb and the other of rats that lived in a ditch in the backyard and somehow got into the house. What terrified him in the latter dream was that the rats looked human. Later in his childhood and for many years afterward Burton had a nightmare in which someone was locked in a coffin, alive. Sometimes Burton was the one locked inside, with his mother standing on the outside, and sometimes this was reversed.

Burton's inability to synthesize contradictory images of objects rendered him, like Atkin's patient, subject to contradictory and incompatible aims. His early development was characterized by both sexual and aggressive overstimulation and trauma. The extent to which his mother was grossly inconsistent, alternately overtly seductive and brutally sadistic, interfered with his ability to synthesize a cohesive image of her. Similarly, the extent to which alternating, extremely intense and incompatible affective states were evoked in him, in the context of profound empathic failures by his mother, interfered with the synthesis of a cohesive self representation. Burton's oscillating suicidal and homicidal preoccupations reflected the fluid interchangeability between images of the self and object as killer and victim. This, along with the rapid fluctuations in his perceptions of the therapist, suggested a developmental arrest at a prestage of splitting (with incomplete self-object differentiation as well). The therapist could discern no defensive purpose underlying these shifting unintegrated representations, nor was there inherent in them any protection of a love object by assigning negative qualities to someone else.

The treatment interventions with this patient were

aimed at stemming the propensity toward decompensation. When the early relationship with his mother was
revived with the therapist, rather than focusing on the
content of his adoration of or rage-filled complaints about
her, she attempted to convey to the patient her empathic
understanding of the intense, alternating, contradictory
feelings to which he was subject and to help him understand the frightening loss of self-cohesion and self-continuity ("imminent disintegration") which he experienced
as a result. Specifically, the therapist addressed herself
to the patient's phase-appropriate need to achieve more
adequate integration, and attempted to provide him with
a model for articulating and synthesizing varying self
and object representations and their associated affects.

FURTHER TREATMENT IMPLICATIONS

Our conceptualization of defenses as endpoints of developmental lines has direct implications for the course of
therapy in the psychoanalytic treatment of patients with
arrests in development. Especially in the early stages of
the analysis of these patients, the analyst will need to
be alert to manifestations of arrests at prestages of defense. As illustrated in our clinical vignettes, when such
manifestations appear, the analyst's interventions will
focus empathically on the states that the patient needs
to maintain or achieve. The analyst's aim here is to promote sufficient structuralization of the representational
world to make possible a subsequent exploration of the
defensive aspects of the patient's psychopathology in
terms of the intrapsychic conflicts it serves to ward off.

The vignettes and case histories described in this
chapter were selected because, in the clinical material,
the manifestations of structural conflict and of arrests in
development were clearly distinguishable. More common

are those patients for whom diagnostic decisions are difficult to make. As we indicated in our discussions of the therapeutic implications of understanding whether a particular pathology connotes a developmental arrest or should be interpreted as a defense, the diagnostic distinction is crucial for the progress of the treatment. A careful judgment about which of the two predominates—and hence, how one should frame the clinical intervention—is required. These evaluations are often difficult to make and are sometimes more accurately understood after the fact than at the requisite moment in treatment. This raises the question of the consequences of an incorrect assessment in either direction. As an example, we might consider two possible approaches to a patient's silence. To accept a patient's silence "empathically" when it is actually serving as a resistance against revealing a "guilty" secret might be contrasted to erroneously interpeting a silence as resistive when it is serving to re-create for the patient a fantasy of merger with an idealized figure, a legitimate developmental need which originally had been interrupted too often and too early. On balance, the consequences that result from misinterpreting the manifestation of an arrested developmental phase as a resistance appear to us to be far graver than the error of misconstruing a resistance as a developmental step.

The failure to analyze a defense is analogous to an incomplete and incorrect interpretation (Glover, 1955) which serves to strengthen resistance. When the analyst interprets as resistive what the patient accurately senses to be a developmental necessity, the patient often experiences the interpretation as a failure of empathy, a breach of trust, a narcissistic injury. It re-creates for the patient a trauma similar to those which originally resulted in the developmental arrest (Balint, 1969; Kohut,

1971). To interpret a defense as a developmental arrest may make the analyst appear at least too benign, at most, Pollyannaish, but generally this can be corrected when a more accurate understanding of the patient's psychic reality is achieved. It may be referred to as a "technical error," as compared to the less forgivable "error in humanity" (Greenson, 1967; Stone, 1961) that comes about through the analyst's failure to acknowledge the validity of a developmental step by dismissing it solely as an aspect of the patient's pathological defenses.

Having emphasized the analytic stance toward developmental arrest that enables the patient to return to and complete the task of consolidating those aspects of self and object representations which have remained vulnerable to regressions, we would like to delineate the clinical criteria which indicate that this "structuralizing" phase of treatment has reached a point where its continuation would undermine the patient's further growth.

Earlier we described the case of Jane to illustrate the extent to which archaic selfobjects were needed for self-esteem regulation. At one point after a prolonged period of symbioticlike, idealizing transference, Jane asked the analyst to say more about himself, to identify himself to her, specifically concerning his views on certain political and social issues. This was seen not primarily as an expression of resistance, but rather as a request for him to assert his existence as a separate object.

Requests like this have been voiced in various forms by numerous similar patients. One young woman reached a comparable point in the third year of her analysis. When she was four her father had left the family, which intensified her attachment to her mother. But this tie was constantly threatened and interrupted by her mother's boyfriend. The separation from her father had revived and exacerbated fears of separation from her mother. The regressively resurgent but prematurely interrupted wishes to merge were covered by a pseudomaturity, but the longings for self-object boundary dissolution remained in the patient's attraction to magical, mystical experiences which provided her with feelings of oneness on a "cosmic" level. In her analysis a symbioticlike transference with a twofold meaning was eventually established. The transference revived the attachment to her mother, although the bond with the analyst was not traumatically disrupted as the tie to her mother had been. The other transference meaning was, "So long as you and I are one with each other, I need not be afraid of your leaving me as my father did." During one session in the third year of the analysis, the patient described a "new feeling" she had recently experienced during sexual intercourse with her boyfriend. She had become particularly and pleasurably aware of the pressure of her friend's body in opposition to her own. Her associations led her to describe similar feelings toward the analyst: she wanted him to make his weight felt more in opposition to her. This wish included her wanting him to introduce new ideas, even ideas contradictory to hers, rather than exploring and clarifying what she was saying. In this instance, an oedipal wish and a developmental step toward self-object differentiation coexisted, and an interpretive response to both was necessary.

At such points in treatment, other patients have described envy of friends who "fight" with their analysts, or they have voiced desires to join a therapy group in order to be subjected to harsher criticism, or a wish that the analyst would describe his views on some sociological or psychoanalytic issue. In each case the pathology of the patient had reflected, to a greater or lesser extent, a developmental arrest and was so treated. These moments marked a turning point in the treatment. The requests did not require fulfillment. The fact that they signaled the patient's readiness for increased tolerance of separation, differences, and opposition had to be recognized. It was also pointed out in each case that, while a step toward self-object separation was in evidence, the patient expected the analyst to differentiate himself from the patient, rather than vice versa. This could now be understood in defensive terms.

From the standpoint of the course of treatment, such a request by a patient is a sign that self-object boundaries have become sufficiently stable so that if the analyst introduces a "new idea"—for example, points out a conflictual wish that the patient is unconsciously defending against—it can now be worked with analytically. Rather than experiencing such interpretations as obliterating, dedifferentiating intrusions, the patient can now react to their content and meaning.

The correct assessment of an arrest at a prestage of defense and the requisite empathic interpretive responses by the analyst gradually enable patients to reach a level at which their representational world becomes sufficiently structured for them to signal the analyst that something "new" is now required of him. The "new" in this case is actually the availability of the patients for a more classical analysis of their structural conflicts and the vicissitudes of their defensive struggles against them.

SUMMARY

In summarizing, a review of the concept of defense reveals that it has remained curiously immune to the impact of recent formulations on the development of self and object representations. We propose that there is a developmental line for each defensive process and that a defense represents the endpoint of a series of developmental achievements. The distinction between psychopathology stemming from defenses against structural conflict and psychopathology rooted in an arrest in representational development at a prestage of defense has decisive diagnostic and therapeutic consequences. While the analytic approach to the former is to interpet what the defending patient needs to ward off, the approach to the latter is to focus empathically on the state which the developmentally arrested patient needs to maintain or achieve. In the treatment of patients with developmental arrests at prestages of defense, the analyst's aim is to promote sufficient structuralization of the representational world to make possible a subsequent, more classical analysis of defenses against intrapsychic conflicts.

Part III

APPLICATIONS AND IMPLICATIONS

7

Death Anxiety, Hypochondriasis, and Depersonalization

In previous chapters, we distinguished the defensive and arrested-developmental aspects of a number of pathological states which have in common a distorted perception of the self or object world. We now extend this conceptualization to an analysis of some frequently occurring phenomena which are of considerable clinical importance—death anxiety, hypochondriasis, and depersonalization. The defensive functions of these states as they arise in the context of intrapsychic conflict will be contrasted with instances in which they signal specific developmental interferences with the articulation and structuralization of the representational world. In these latter instances, the predominant focus will be upon the self representation, its inadequate consolidation, and the deficiencies in its structural cohesion and temporal stability that render it vulnerable to regressive dissolution. A consideration of other states of consciousness (e.g., derealization) in which the accent falls more upon the object world than upon the self would bring to focus analogous developmental failures in the consolidation of object representations.

DEATH ANXIETY AND HYPOCHONDRIASIS

A survey of the literature on death anxiety (Stolorow, 1973) reveals that it is a multifaceted, multiply deter-, mined phenomenon, subject to a wide range of interpretations by authors of varying theoretical schools. Classically, death anxiety has been interpreted as an expression of a variety of unconscious infantile fears—of castration (Freud, 1923; Bromberg and Schilder, 1933), of separation or object loss (Bromberg and Schilder, 1936), of one's own overwhelming sexual excitement or masochistic, self-destructive urges (Fenichel, 1945), and of talionic punishments and persecutions issuing from unconscious guilt (Freud, 1923; Bromberg and Schilder, 1936).

These interpretations have several points in common. First, death anxiety is assumed to be a vicissitude of infantile conflict. Second, death anxiety is seen as partially expressing, but also as defensively disguising, an unconscious infantile fear. A dreaded infantile danger situation is replaced, through displacements, projections, and other defensive operations, with a presumably more tolerable threat to life and limb. And third, the meaning of death anxiety tends to be linked with a concomitant of the dying process (mutilation, pain, loss, etc.) rather than to the extinction of existence per se (Bromberg and Schilder, 1933).

Closely allied both phenomenologically and conceptually to death anxiety is the syndrome of hypochondriasis. As Rosenfeld (1964a) suggests, Freud's (1914a) early conception of hypochondriasis as an "actual neurosis" may have hindered the elucidation of its meanings and functions. Freud theorized that hypochondriacal anxiety is essentially a physiological by-product of narcissistic withdrawal—the detachment of libido from the outer world and its redirection onto the self. When this redirected libido cannot be psychically mastered through megalomanic fantasy, it becomes dammed up and, in turn, must be partially discharged in the form of hypochondriacal anxiety. Thus, hypochondriacal anxiety results from the damming up of narcissistic libido, just as neurotic anxiety derives from the damming up of object libido. His argument rested upon his early economic concept of anxiety as an automatic physiological consequence of repression.

Following his creation of the structural theory, Freud (1926) revised his concept of anxiety and viewed it as an affect generated to signal anticipated intrapsychic danger and the need for defense. Yet he did not update his view on hypochondriasis to conform to the newer signal theory, and a number of subsequent authors—e.g., Nunberg (1932) and Fenichel (1945)—continued to hold to the old economic concept of hypochondriacal states. Nonetheless, these authors also provided interpretations of hypochondriacal anxiety closely similar to those which have been offered for death anxiety, interpreting it as an expression of castration fear, of destructive wishes turned away from an object onto one's own organs (which represent the incorporated object), and of a sense of guilt and need/fear of talionic punishments. As with the formulations of death anxiety, these interpretations of hypochondriacal states stress their defensive function in disguising various components of infantile conflict.

An emphasis on defenses, especially the very primitive ones, is particularly characteristic of Kleinian interpretations of hypochondriacal anxiety. Melanie Klein (1935), for example, viewed hypochondriacal symptoms as the product of fantasies of attacks by internalized persecutory objects against the self (paranoid position) or of wishes to save good internalized objects from attacks by bad ones and by the self (depressive position). According to Rosenfeld (1964a), hypochondriasis stems from the splitting off of oral-sadistic parts of the self and internal objects and their projection into external objects which are in turn immediately reincorporated into the body and body organs.

These and similar formulations by Kleinian analysts underscore the role of primitive forms of defensive projection, incorporation, and splitting in the genesis of hypochondriacal states. In the previous chapters, we have stressed that the active use of such mental operations for defensive purposes presupposes the attainment of certain developmental milestones. For example, the defensive translocation of psychic contents across self-object boundaries, as in projection and incorporation, requires that those boundaries have been at least partially consolidated. Similarly, a defensive split into parts requires a prior integration of a whole. These developmental requirements cannot be assumed to have been accomplished in all cases of hypochondriasis, particularly in patients with borderline or psychotic personalities. In such cases, hypochondriacal anxiety might arise, for example, as one aspect of a state of self-object confusion which is the remnant of an arrest in development at an early prestage of projection and incorporation characterized by an inability to adequately differentiate self and object images. Rosenfeld (1964a) seemed to be alluding to a somewhat similar point in stressing the importance of archaic confusional states in hypochondriasis, but he did not distinguish the defensive and arrested developmental aspects of this confusion.

An examination of the signal function of hypochondriacal anxiety may serve as a springboard for exploring the arrested-developmental aspects of both hypochondriasis and death anxiety. Freud's (1914a) early notion of the parallel between the role of neurotic anxiety in the transference neuroses and hypochondriacal anxiety in the narcissistic disturbances can be updated and amplified in the light of his later signal theory of anxiety (1926). Specifically, just as neurotic anxiety signals anticipated dangers emanating from object love and object hate, hypochondriacal anxiety may signal an endangered sense of self. Hence, hypochondriacal anxiety takes its place among such affects as self-consciousness, embarrassment, shame, and humiliation in signaling threats to the self representation, in contrast to those affects (e.g., castration anxiety and guilt) which signal the emergence of structural conflicts (Jacobson, 1964; Kohut, 1971).

This formulation of the signal function of hypochondriacal anxiety sheds light on the finding that hypochondriacal worries frequently make their appearance during adolescence and middle age. The threats posed to the integrity of the self representation by its massive reorganizations during the regressive and progressive shifts of adolescence have been well documented (Blos, 1962). As to middle age, Kernberg (1975) has commented on the devastating effect that aging can have on the narcissistic personality, in forcing " . . . the eventual confrontation of the grandiose self with the frail, limited and transitory nature of human life" (p. 311). In either case, hypochondriacal anxiety may sound the alarm, signaling looming threats to the cohesion, stability, and affective coloring of the self representation, and the urgent need for narcissistic restoration.

In keeping with Freud's (1914a) observation that hypochondriacal spells may foreshadow severe narcissistic decompensation, Kohut (1971) has suggested that hypochondriacal states may specifically signal the impending danger of structural fragmentation and disintegration of the self representation through a regressive preoccupation with isolated body parts and mental functions (e.g., in the wake of narcissistic injuries or disruptions in a narcissistically sustaining transference situation). This formulation brings the signal concept of hypochondriacal anxiety into close relation with the notion of developmental arrest, since the danger of a regressive dissolution of the self representation can occur only on the basis of its insufficient articulation and consolidation during the early formative years. Indeed, Kohut's clinical illustrations all point to the emergence of hypochondriacal worries in the context of an extreme structural vulnerability of the self representation, viewed as a remnant of developmental arrests at archaic selfobject configurations. This developmental formulation is also confirmed in the well-known cases of the Wolf Man and Schreber, which illustrate the role of hypochondriacal anxiety, triggered by threats to the self representation, in signaling incipient narcissistic decompensations (see Brunswick, 1928; Niederland, 1951).

Kohut (1971) has also discovered that when certain developmentally arrested patients become able, as a result of analytic progress, to immerse themselves in novel pursuits and activities, they may at first experience such immersion as posing a threat of self-loss, a danger signaled by transitory hypochondriacal states. Two closely related observations can be made in working with patients when developmentally arrested configurations have been analyzed. Such patients tend to react to each recognition of progress in their analysis with mild hypochondriacal concerns, sometimes accompanied by fleeting feelings of self-estrangement. Classically, such occurrences might be interpreted as the product of a sense of guilt evoked by the awareness of progress, which is unconsciously equated with an oedipal triumph. While such formulations are undoubtedly correct in some in-

stances, for narcissistically arrested patients the awareness of progress and, hence, of change in themselves may
constitute a threat to the stability of their self representation, to their sense of self-continuity or identity. The
emergence of this threat, along with a sense of the fragility of the newly reorganized self representation, may
be signaled by the appearance of hypochondriacal worries.

The second observation concerns hypochondriacal
spells which come about when patients begin to experience a depth or intensity in their object relations of which
they heretofore had been incapable. One such patient
began to brood about a felt inadequacy in her memory
function (mental hypochondriasis) when, at age 35, she
was for the first time able to become passionately involved in a love affair. Her hypochondriacal preoccupation with her memory signaled and concretized the
specific threat to her inadequately consolidated sense of
self-continuity posed by her wishes to merge with her
idealized lover.

As with hypochondriasis, death anxiety too may signal threats to the cohesion and stability of a self representation rendered vulnerable and fragile by developmental interferences with its structuralization—a
formulation to which Rank (1929) and Guntrip (1969)
have also alluded. This might be particularly true when
the content of the death anxiety pertains more to the
state of being dead (extinction of existence, nothingness,
nonbeing) than to the various accompaniments of the
dying process. Such feelings of "existential dread," in
signaling the impending danger of self-dissolution, may
be viewed as an analogue to psychotic fantasies of world
destruction, which foreshadow the loss of the subjective
object world (Freud, 1911b, 1914a). As we shall see, this
type of death anxiety bears a close relation to states of

depersonalization in developmentally arrested patients, just as world-destruction fantasies often coincide with states of derealization.

An illustration of the intimate connections between the occurrence of death anxiety and the precariousness of an insufficiently consolidated self representation can be found in an analysis of the life and work of Otto Rank (Stolorow and Atwood, 1976). During his early childhood Rank suffered massive, shattering, repetitive narcissistic traumata in the areas of both the grandiose self and the idealized parent imago (Kohut, 1971)—developmental traumata that seriously interfered with the structuralization of his self representation. His vulnerability to narcissistic decompensations (including severe episodes of hypochondriasis and depersonalization) as well as his continual confrontation with the danger of self-fragmentation and self-dissolution were both signaled and concretized by an acute and preoccupying terror of death, which plagued him since he had been a young child and which became the leitmotif of his theoretical work.

Particularly persuasive confirmations of the developmental conception of death anxiety can be found in those patients in whom it appears as a direct result of developmental processes set in motion in the course of psychoanalytic treatment. This seemed to be the case with Bill, a patient whose therapy was discussed in the previous chapter. Central to his disorder was his extreme narcissistic vulnerability, rooted in a developmental failure to consolidate a cohesive, stable, and positively colored self representation. He ceaselessly strove to sustain a spurious sense of self-cohesion, self-continuity, and self-esteem by maintaining a fantasied identity between the performance of his actual self and the image of a grandiose, invincibly omnipotent, and exquisitely flawless wishful self. Any circumstance that dramatized the discrepancy between his actual self and grandiose wishful self led to feelings of searing shame, intense humiliation, merciless self-hatred and, most catastrophically, to an experience of self-fragmentation and self-dissolution (sometimes accompanied by depersonalization). Early in the treatment he attempted to restore his sense of self-cohesion in the face of such injurious experiences by indulging in primitive, perverse, sadomasochistic, and exhibitionistic fantasies and acts.

In concert with the unveiling of his narcissistic pathology, the patient was gradually able to form, in relation to the analyst, a stable narcissistic transference of the mirroring type (Kohut, 1971) and thereby increasingly experienced a buttressing of his fragile self representation. As a result of the uncovering, partial working through, and gradual tempering of his grandiose fantasies and expectations within the transference, toward the end of the fourth year of analysis he began to show evidence of having acquired the beginnings of a cohesive, autonomously maintained self representation. Correspondingly, narcissistic insults no longer evoked states of total self-disintegration, and hence the florid pathological fantasies and acts which earlier had served a narcissistic function in restoring his crumbling self representation were no longer necessary and faded into the background. During this same period, however, he began to experience an acute dread of death, centering on the idea of the extinction of his existence. According to his recollections, it was the first time that he had either feared death or confronted its inevitability.

The emergence of death anxiety in this patient undoubtedly had multiple meanings, including some of those reviewed earlier in this chapter. For one thing, the inevitability of his eventual death (the ultimate narcissistic injury), which might strike him down at any moment, represented perhaps the most serious challenge yet to his grandiose self. However, the patient and analyst also came to understand that the appearance of the fear of death at this juncture in the patient's treatment was a direct consequence of his having achieved an important developmental milestone. The appearance of death anxiety was an "indicator" (Spitz, 1959) of his having attained a firmer structuralization of his self representation. Prior to this achievement, the experience of acute death anxiety had been largely beyond the scope of his capacities, since he lacked the representation of an integrated and valued self that would be lost as a result of his death. With the beginning establishment of a cohesive, stable, and positively colored self representation, the experience of death anxiety had become a possibility. He now felt, perhaps for the first time, that he had a self to lose.

The acuteness of Bill's dread and the urgency of his preoccupation with death were clearly a measure of the precariousness of his newly germinated sense of self. Yet it would have been a breach of empathy had the analyst focused only on the pathological implications of the death fear, rather than recognizing with the patient that his anxiety was a manifestation of a pivotal developmental achievement.

DEPERSONALIZATION

As with death anxiety and hypochondriasis, depersonalization—the uncanny sense of estrangement from or feeling of unreality about the bodily or mental self—has been subject to a wide range of interpretation. Those authors who held to an economic concept of hypochondriasis also tended to include the notion of detachment from external objects in their explanations of depersonalization (Nunberg, 1924; Fenichel, 1945). However, as was also the case with death anxiety and hypochondriasis, most classical interpretations of depersonalization have in common an emphasis upon its defensive function in warding off various components of infantile conflict.

Freud (1919b) attributed feelings of uncanniness, in part, to the return of repressed infantile conflicts and later (1936) asserted that depersonalization and derealization serve the purpose of defense in aiming to repudiate something that threatens to stir forbidden infantile strivings. In various other formulations, depersonalization has been seen to defensively repudiate or ward off bodily sensations and feelings which evoke guilt (Nunberg, 1932; Oberndorf, 1950); anal exhibitionistic promptings (Bergler and Eidelberg, 1935); heightened sexual interest in one's own bodily organs or mental processes (Fenichel, 1945); primitive destructive urges, depression, and persecutory feelings (Rosenfeld, 1947); anxieties arising from oral deprivation and rage (Blank, 1954); indentifications with degraded or conflicting sadomasochistically tinged object images (Jacobson, 1971, ch. 5; Sarlin, 1962); and powerful sexual and aggressive wishes of all levels (Stamm, 1962).

An example of this classical emphasis upon the defensive function is found in the analysis of depersonalization provided by Arlow (1966). Depersonalization, says Arlow, involves a defensive splitting of the self representation which dissociates a participating self from an observing self in the context of severe intrapsychic conflict. The patient attributes the warded-off wishes and danger situation to a participating self, which he experiences as estranged. Essentially, depersonalization involves an unconscious defensive fantasy in which a dangerous intrapsychic conflict is conceived as belonging to a stranger rather than the self. As for the meaning of the anxiety which often accompanies the depersonalization experience, Arlow stresses that the patient is not anxious because he feels depersonalized; rather, he feels depersonalized because he wishes to ward off an anxiety-arousing danger. We will evaluate this latter assertion later in this chapter. For now, two comments on Arlow's contribution: First, a defensive splitting of the self representation presupposes its prior integration, a presupposition that may not hold true for certain developmentally arrested depersonalized patients. Second, some of the clinical data and formulations provided by Arlow and other authors can be shown to contain evidence of interference and arrests along a number of developmental lines, a point which we now take up in detail.

From a survey of the literature and clinical material to be described, four closely related and overlapping developmental lines emerge that have particular relevance to the problem of depersonalization. It can be argued that these four are in reality facets of a single developmental line, or perhaps descriptions of the same line in different terms or from different points of view. However, they tend to appear separately in the literature and so we will present them as such, if only for heuristic purposes.

Sleeping to Waking Consciousness

The close similarity between depersonalization experiences and the states of sleep and dreaming has been noted by numerous authors (Nunberg, 1924; Rosenfeld, 1947; Blank, 1954; Stamm, 1962; Arlow, 1966; Levitan, 1967, 1969, 1970). Indeed, Blank (1954) and Stamm (1962) have described depersonalization as a defensive regression to a hypnagogic, sleeplike, or dreamlike state and Levitan (1967, 1969, 1970) has suggested that depersonalization occurs when certain sensation-deadening and affect-abrogating dream mechanisms persist from deep sleep into the waking state. Levitan has supported his suggestion with detailed clinical illustrations.

These observations and formulations may be brought into a developmental framework through Bach's (1977) proposal that the ontogenetic progression from early states of consciousness characteristic of sleep to adult waking consciousness may be viewed as a developmental achievement, one which is incompletely attained by certain patients. Indeed, many of the cases described by the authors just mentioned lend support to the idea that arrests along this particular developmental line can contribute to a propensity for experiences of depersonalization, particularly those with a dreamlike quality. The frequent concurrence of dreamlike depersonalized states with the triad of wishes to sleep, to devour, and to be devoured, sometimes coupled with primitive intrauterine and merger fantasies (Rosenfeld, 1947; Lewin, 1950; Blank, 1954; Stamm, 1962; Levitan, 1967, 1969), points to the intimate connection of the sleeping-waking dimension with the vicissitudes of self-object separation. Furthermore, as Bach (1977) has pointed out, the line of development from sleeping to waking consciousness is closely related to the progression from archaic narcissism to a firmly established reflective self-awareness. As we shall see, interferences with this latter developmental progression, as well as with the achievement of self-object differentiation, also play an important role in the genesis of depersonalization.

Self-Object Differentiation

We noted that the clinical illustrations offered by a number of authors who stress the defensive function of depersonalization contain evidence for the contribution of primitive intrauterine and merger fantasies to the de-

personalization experience. Guntrip (1969) explicitly attributed depersonalization in schizoid patients to
experiences of self-dissolution which accompany deeply
regressive states of withdrawal into intrauterine fantasies. While these primitive states and fantasies can be
interpreted as the product of defensive regressions, they
also point to the role of arrests in the development of self-
object differentiation in predisposing a person to depersonalized states. A similar conclusion can be drawn from
those observations which stress the operation of primitive
identifications, or defenses against them, in the origins
of depersonalization (Sarlin, 1962; Jacobson, 1971, ch. 5).

Federn (1952) was perhaps the first psychoanalyst to
specifically relate states of estrangement and depersonalization to developmental impairments in self-object
boundaries and defects in the sense of self-coherence.
Mahler (1960) has demonstrated that, in certain psychotic children, states of estrangement may be rooted in
an impairment of the capacity to discriminate the human
object world (including the self) from the inanimate environment (see Spitz, 1963).

As was the case with death anxiety and hypchon-
driasis, the developmental hypothesis finds confirmation
in a case in which episódes of depersonalization were
evoked by developmental processes set in motion by the
analysis. When Mary began her treatment at the age of
30, she had been rendered nearly homebound by multiple,
severe agoraphobic symptoms. Prominent in her personality disorder were sexual inhibitions, depressive and
dependent trends, and a pervasive narcissistic vulnerability which contributed to her extreme self-consciousness and frequent, searing feelings of shame,
embarrassment, and self-hatred. The extent to which her
sexual and agoraphobic difficulties were rooted in a masochistic, symbioticlike bond to an invasive, sadistically

controlling and binding mother (see Frances and Dunn, 1975) was dramatically depicted in a dream in which an older woman was cutting out a young girl's vagina so that the girl would remain with her rather than venture out to have relations with men. Interferences with self-object differentiation were shown in the immediate, total "empathy" she experienced for the feeling states of her mother and mother surrogates, and in the silent, trance-like, mystical mergings with the idealized analyst that she experienced early in the treatment.

During the first two years of the analysis, Mary gradually became immersed in a stable narcissistic transference with both mirroring and idealizing components. During this period, the contribution of her narcissistic disturbance to her agoraphobic symptoms was systematically explored—for example, her fears of exposing humiliating weaknesses and evoking unendurable ridicule while "trapped in the spotlight." The origins of these fears were in turn traced to repeated early traumata in which her independent grandiose-exhibitionistic strivings and her actual accomplishments were consistently met by her mother with complete unresponsiveness, undermining belittlement, or relentless criticism, thereby discouraging intrapsychic separation and strengthening the masochistic, symbioticlike bond.

As a result of the solidification of the transference and the insights gained during this period of the therapy, Mary achieved a marked improvement in her agoraphobic symptoms and began to engage in a variety of autonomous activities which previously had been unimaginable to her. However, with each successful mastery of a new activity she experienced a transitory spell of depersonalization. She described an uncanny feeling of unreality, as if the activity were being performed by someone else, a stranger, not herself.

While there were certainly defensive components in these depersonalized states, they were seen primarily to reflect a crucial developmental step in self-object differentiation (see Paul and Carson, 1976), and were so interpreted to the patient. Mary became depersonalized, in part, because each independent performance of a novel activity constituted an experience of intrapsychic separation from her mother and mother surrogates (husband, analyst) and, hence, a beginning loss of her "symbiotic identity" (Caldwell, 1976). At the same time, her newly differentiating self was most precarious and indeed seemed like a stranger to her. During a later phase in treatment, after considerable structuralization of her representational world had been accomplished, she again began to experience spells of depersonalization, this time in the context of oedipal conflicts surfacing in the transference. Now the depersonalizations were understood and interpreted as defensive repudiations of her conflictual transference wishes, in a manner similar to that described by Arlow (1966).

Psychosomatic Indwelling

Closely related to both self-object separation and the development of a cohesive self is the acquisition of a state of awareness which Winnicott (1945, 1962) has referred to as "personalization" or "psychosomatic indwelling" and which Elkin (1972) has called "embodied selfhood." With the achievement of indwelling, the skin becomes the subjective boundary between the self and the object world and, experientially, the psyche has come to reside within the soma. Developmental contributions to this localization of the unit self within the body are made by the proper holding and handling of the child's body (Winnicott, 1945, 1962), by the sensual stimulations of the child's body surface within the early mother-child relationship (Hoffer, 1950; Mahler et al., 1975), and by a variety of early mirror and mirrorlike experiences (Lacan, 1949; Elkish, 1957; Winnicott, 1967; Kohut, 1971). According to Winnicott (1945, 1962), depersonalization may specifically result from failures to attain this sense of psychosomatic unity as a consequence of developmental interferences and lags.

A dramatic illustration of such a developmental failure is found in the case described by Atwood (1977) of a nineteen-year-old woman who was convinced that she possessed a group of extraordinary paranormal powers. Most notably, she reported experiences in which her mind traveled out of her body and invisibly observed other people far removed from her in space—a rupture in mind-body unity which caricatures that found in depersonalization.

Both parents of this patient appeared to have been deeply disturbed people who showed little interest in her except to use her parasitically as an extension of their own narcissistic needs and as a scapegoat for their own disappointments and misfortunes. Hence, her early life was marked by an absence of empathic mirroring, by devastating feelings of rejection, and by frequent sadistic beatings at the hands of both parents. The patient often thought they hated her and wished her dead, and for several years of her childhood she entertained terrifying fantasies of being gruesomely murdered in her sleep. Significantly, she remembered that when she was about two and a half the parents decided that she was too old to be hugged and cuddled and abruptly terminated all such body contact.

The patient traced her ability to project herself out of her body to a series of visitations when she was five years old, in which the benign ghosts of two dead grandparents lifted her from her body and transported her to a place called "the field," a peaceful, completely isolated expanse of grass and trees where she could feel totally secure and protected from the human object world. Thereafter, she became able to project herself to the field voluntarily and, eventually, to travel anywhere in an invisible disembodied form. The out-of-body experiences increased in frequency at age seven, when she developed a brain tumor which caused agonizing headaches, and which was not correctly diagnosed and removed until she was ten.

In the light of this patient's traumatic early history and the severe, primitive object-related conflicts from which she suffered as a consequence, the defensive and restitutive functions of her quasi-delusional journeys are readily apparent. Yet it also seems safe to conclude that the lack of parental mirroring, the literal failure of the "holding environment" in abruptly withdrawing all affectionate body contact, and the frequent, brutal beatings (and later, the headaches) whereby the patient came to experience her bruised body as an alien, intruding source of perpetual pain, constituted massive developmental impediments interfering with the integration of her mental and bodily selves. Indeed, as early as age three she had already become obsessed with questions about how her mind could make her body parts move—questions that signaled the specific developmental arrest in the attainment of psychosomatic indwelling. In her psychotherapeutic treatment, the symbolic holding provided by the therapist's empathic attunement to her primitive representational world seemed much more effective in decreasing her paranormal experiences than were interpretations of their defensive functions.

Archaic Narcissism to Self-Constancy

Already implied in the lines of development discussed so

far is the ontogenetic progression, elucidated by Kohut (1971, 1977), from the archaic narcissistic configurations to the achievement of a cohesive, stable, and postively colored self-representation. It will therefore come as no surprise that interferences with this developmental progression are strongly implicated in predisposing a person to depersonalization experiences.

Kohut (1971), for example, has presented several clinical illustrations in which depersonalizationlike feelings of inner deadness and self-estrangement accompanied the regressive fragmentation of an insufficiently structuralized and vulnerable self representation in narcissistically arrested patients. The case of Bill, described earlier in connection with death anxiety, provides an additional example of this phenomenon. Fast and Chethik (1976) have shown that depersonalization may occur in narcissistically disturbed children in consequence of the loss of a selfobject whose function had been to validate the reality of self-experience. Here, depersonalization was the remnant of a specific failure in internalization.

A number of descriptions of depersonalized patients highlight defects in that component of self-constancy which pertains to the temporal stability of the self representation—the sense of self-continuity or identity. For example, the case material presented by Jacobson (1971, ch. 5) and Sarlin (1962) emphasized their patients' severe identity disturbances rooted in developmental failures to internalize and integrate conflicting object images and an absence of acceptable models for idealization and identification. In these patients, many of whom were reminiscent of "as-if" (Deutsch, 1942) or "false self" (Winnicott, 1960) personalities, depersonalized states were evoked by experiences which constituted ruptures in their precarious sense of self-continuity, of "going-on-being" (Winnicott, 1962). Bach (1975), in particular, has interpreted a variety of uncanny experiences, including depersonalization, as reflecting disjunctions in the self-experience rooted in a narcissistic developmental deficit which includes a lack of belief in the continuity and substantiality of the self (see also Frances et al., 1977). This deficit, seen as resulting from early failures in the mother's mirroring function (Kohut, 1971) or repeated derailments of the mother-child dialogue (Spitz, 1964), becomes apparent in the analytic situation when uncanny, depersonalized states are triggered by disruptions in a narcissistic transference.

Two cases will briefly illustrate the contribution of arrested narcissistic development to the depersonalization experience. When James began his treatment at the age of 31, he described a history of tormenting, sadomasochistic entanglements with cold, self-engrossed, unresponsive women. Experiences in which these women failed to recognize his needs and feelings ushered in highly disturbing foglike states of depersonalization. He was able in the analysis to trace the inception of these foglike states to his mother's breakdown with a psychotic depression when he was five years old. Thereafter, his needs for maternal empathy and a mirroring response to his blossoming phallic grandiosity were met with his mother's stony withdrawal into depressive self-absorption. While the defensive functions of his foglike states were readily discernible (e.g., in warding off murderous rage at his icy, unresponsive mother and her surrogates), they seemed primarily the product of the massive traumatic depletion of his phallic grandiosity by his mother's empathic failures and of the consequent developmental interference with the consolidation of his self representation. Hence, he felt his vulnerable self crumble and dissolve in a soupy fog whenever the object world failed to confirm his emotional existence.

James was gradually able to establish a stable mirror transference with the analyst, which reinstated the developmental processes that had been abruptly aborted by his mother's depressive withdrawals. During this period of the treatment he made use of a tape recorder in an interesting manner which proved to be highly therapeutic. In the wake of mortifications and disappointments, he would record his feelings on tape, and then listen to the recording with the same empathic, understanding attitude he had experienced from the analyst. This use of the tape recorder as a transitional selfobject, which signaled a partial internalization of the analyst's mirror function, enabled him to regain a sense of conviction about his own substantiality and helped him to restore self-cohesion in the wake of narcissistic injuries. It enabled him to feel increasingly real and alive and eventually to acquire a deep empathy and respect for his own damaged self. The foglike depersonalized states of self-fragmentation completely lifted. Interestingly, he became able at this time to feel his deep rage at his mother and her surrogates without the defensive function of the depersonalizations ever having been interpreted. And like Bill, James also began to experience a heightened awareness of himself as a mortal being.

In the second example, the analysis of a dream elucidated the meaning of a depersonalized state which was evoked by the transference. George, a 27-year-old dancer, sought psychoanalytic help for the severe disturbances in self-esteem regulation which impeded his work. Prior to one of his sessions early in the treatment, he had eagerly anticipated telling the analyst about how well he was performing at his rehearsals. However, during the session itself he felt "outside" of himself; he felt he was reporting on his good performance in a mechanical, lifeless manner. His associations to this state included the

following recurrent dream, which contained a representation of a depersonalized state in its manifest content:

> I'm in a pit. It's very deep and very bright, so you can't see
> where the wall meets the floor. I'm getting good responses,
> people are applauding. Then it turns into jeering and
> booing. At some point someone throws me a ladder. I climb
> up over the edge, and there's nothing there, no audience,
> just blackness, only the noise of the jeering and booing. I
> look back down into the void. Then I see myself at the edge
> of the pit looking down at the void. I go back and forth
> between looking down into the void and seeing myself
> looking.

The patient's associations to the pit enabled him to
remember several psychoticlike states suffered when he
was seven years old, in which he was plagued by terrifying, quasi-delusional images of being mutilated and
cut up by trolls who resided first in a big hole near his
house and later under his bed. His parents emerged in
his memories as shadowy, distant, self-engrossed people
who used George's considerable talents to find fulfillment
of their own dreams of glory. He could recall only one
instance of physical contact with a parent: his mother
hugged him at his father's funeral when he was seven-
teen.

It was inferred from this and other material that
George came to rely on experiences of being looked at,
admired, and applauded as a substitute for the affectionate holding and warm body contact of which he was mas-
sively deprived (see Kohut, 1971). As a result of this
developmental distortion, his sense of self-cohesion and
self-continuity became almost completely dependent on
his finding confirmations from the object world for his
grandiose-exhibitionistic strivings. As shown in the
dream, depersonalized states arose in reaction to real and
imagined mortifications, both as an expression of and a

protection from the dangerous, regressive decompensations (the deep, bottomless void) to which his precariously consolidated self was vulnerable when the vitally needed narcissistic confirmation was absent.

CONCLUSIONS

In this chapter it was shown that death anxiety, hypochondriasis, and depersonalization may occur, in developmentally arrested patients, as symptoms of deficiencies in the consolidation of a structurally cohesive and temporally stable self representation. In their arrested developmental aspects, death anxiety, hypochondriasis, and depersonalization were revealed to be closely related to one another along a continuum of degrees or stages of narcissistic decompensation. All three clinical states are evoked by the specter of a fragmenting or disintegrating self representation. Death anxiety occurs as a signal when self-fragmentation is merely anticipated as a threatening possibility. Hypochondriasis sounds the alarm when the regressive self-disintegration has actually begun and the preoccupation with bodily organs or mental functions already contains a concretizing effort at self-stabilization and self-restitution. In depersonalization, the process of self-dissolution has proceeded even further and is directly represented in the uncanny feeling that the self has become unreal or estranged. Additional decompensation would lead to psychotic disorganization.

We are now in a position to reexamine the meaning of the anxiety which often accompanies the depersonalization experience. Arlow's (1966) assertion, that the patient is not anxious because he feels depersonalized but feels depersonalized because he wishes to ward off anxiety, can now be seen to apply only in those instances where the depersonalization is primarily the product of

defensive activity. In structurally deficient, developmentally arrested patients the anxiety is inherent in the
depersonalization state itself and reflects the person's
rock-bottom terror in experiencing the fragmentation
and disintegration of his very self. Indeed, a person may
resort to a variety of primitive, perverse, sadomasochistic, and exhibitionistic fantasies and acts in an effort to
counteract this frightening experience of depersonalization and self-loss. Such was the case with Bill prior to the
self-consolidation that occurred as a result of treatment.
In line with our formulation pertaining to degrees of narcissistic decompensation, it is noteworthy that Bill's depersonalization experiences and primitive restitutive
efforts were gradually supplanted by episodes of death
anxiety as his self representation acquired greater structuralization and became less vulnerable to regressive
fragmentation.

Death anxiety, hypochondriasis, and depersonalization, like all complex mental phenomena, have multiple
origins and serve multiple functions (Waelder, 1936). In
any given occurrence of one or another of these symptoms,
it is the clinical task to determine the motivational priority or urgency of the different functions it may be serving
for a particular patient at a particular point in the treatment (Stolorow et al., 1978). As we have shown, it is
especially important to assess whether the symptom is
primarily serving the purposes of defense or whether it
is more accurately understood as reflecting deficiencies
in the structuralization of the self representation as a
remnant of a developmental arrest at a prestage of defense.

The therapeutic implications of making such distinctions have already been discussed. In the case of death
anxiety, hypochrondriasis, or depersonalization which is
rooted in a developmental arrest, the analyst's goal in

framing his interventions is to promote the structuralization of the self representation. This, in turn, may make possible a subsequent exploration of the symptom's defensive functions in terms of the intrapsychic conflicts it serves to ward off.

8

Sexual Fantasy and Perverse Activity

In this chapter we explore the reciprocal relationship between sexual fantasies and acts, on the one hand, and the structuralization of self and object representations, on the other. That early sensual experiences contribute significantly to the *content* of self and object representations has long been known to clinical psychoanalysts, beginning with Freud (1905b, 1927). Here, we are concerned primarily with the role of psychosexuality in determining certain *formal properties* of the representational world—i.e., with the function of sensual experiences, fantasies, and enactments in consolidating the structural cohesion and temporal stability of self and object representations, both in the course of normal development and, abortively, in adult sexual perversions. Conversely, we discuss the ways in which particular psychosexual imagery may signal developmental steps in the consolidation of self and object representations.

PSYCHOSEXUALITY AND NORMAL
REPRESENTATIONAL DEVELOPMENT

To elucidate systematically the contribution of psychosexual phases to the structuralization of self and object representations in the course of normal development would require the construction of a comprehensive developmental psychology of the representational world supported by data from detailed empirical research. We offer, instead, a brief review of some relevant contributions to the analytic literature and some formulations based on existent theory.

George Klein (1976) suggested that, from the standpoint of clinical theory, sexuality must always be understood in terms of a developing self that seeks "to perpetuate and preserve its unity, integrity, and coherence" (p. 94). A number of analysts have commented more or less extensively on the role of phase-appropriate psychosexual experiences in articulating and consolidating various facets of the self representation for the normally developing child. According to Jacobson (1964), each stage of psychosexual development makes its own unique contributions to the development of ego and superego functions and, by implication, to both the content and formal properties of the evolving self representation. Greenacre (1958) stresses the importance of early psychosexual experiences, particularly those involving the genitals, in establishing the child's recognition of his body self. Emphasizing the earlier pregenital phase, Hoffer (1950) and Mahler et al. (1975) claim that the delineation of a rudimentary body image is accomplished through the sensual stimulations of the child's body surface resulting from pleasurable contacts within the mother-infant interactions. In a similar vein, Winnicott (1945, 1962) believed that the proper (sensual) holding and handling of the infant gives rise to the attainment of "psychosomatic indwelling," a state of awareness in which the child experiences himself as a unit located within his body and bounded by his skin. Lichtenstein (1961) proposes that through the primitive pregenital sensual stimulations that occur within the early mother-child unit, the infant is "imprinted" with the most basic outlines for the development of his identity. And finally, Kohut (1971, 1977) believes that the child's exhibitionistic and voyeuristic pursuits, if met with empathic, phase-appropriate parental responsiveness, contribute crucially to the gradual transformation of archaic narcissistic configurations into a mature sense of self-cohesion, self-continuity, and self-esteem.

Erikson's (1950) distinction between psychosexual *zones* and psychosexual *modes* provides us with an important conceptual advance in our efforts to comprehend the role of sensual experiences and fantasies in articulating the developing child's representational world. The epigenetic unfolding of psychosexual modes can be shown to serve in critical ways the consolidation of an individualized representation of the self, which is differentiated from images of primary objects. Such structuralization, in turn, makes possible new modes of psychosexual experience, so that the occurrence of particular psychosexual imagery may signal a developmental step in the consolidation of self and object representations. We are suggesting that each psychosexual phase can best be understood in terms of this reciprocal interplay between sensual and representational development.

Experiences and fantasies in the oral-incorporative mode contribute to the process of self-object differentiation by affirming the subjective distinction between inside and outside, between the self as a container and the nonself which can be taken in. At the same time, the child may employ incorporative fantasies to appropriate valued and admired qualities of objects to his own self representation, contributing further to its eventual structuralization (Jacobson, 1964; Kohut, 1971).

Conversely, oral imagery, though frequently viewed

in terms of dependency wishes, can also be seen as signaling the attainment of rudimentary self-object boundaries. Oral-incorporative fantasies imply that at least a germinal distinction between the devouring self and the object to be devoured has been achieved. Hence, oral imagery stands in contrast to symbiotic fantasy, since the latter embodies the archaic undifferentiated self-object unit. Viewed this way, it becomes apparent that oral-incorporative and symbiotic merging fantasies reflect different degrees of structuralization of self and object representations.

Experiences and fantasies in the anal-retentive mode provide a stubborn affirmation of the boundaries separating self and nonself, a definitive milestone in self-object differentiation. Through anal-eliminative acts and fantasies, the child ejects undesirable contents from his self representation, further promoting its individualization and refining its demarcation from the object world (Kohut, 1977). At the same time, the appearance of anal imagery signals that self-object boundaries have been sufficiently consolidated so that, henceforth, aggression can be used in the service of further intrapsychic separation.

A particularly decisive step in self-definition occurs with the discovery of genital differences (see Grossman and Stewart, 1976) and the unfolding of the intrusive and inclusive genital modes which begin to distinguish the sensual self-experience of boys and girls respectively. As with oral-incorporative and anal-aggressive fantasies, phallic imagery too can serve to buttress the vulnerable self representations of developing children of both sexes (see A. Reich, 1953, 1960; Jacobson, 1964; Kohut, 1971, 1977). The oedipal saga itself may be viewed as a pivotal phase in the structuralization of the self (Kohut, 1977), which finds its fatefully unique form in emerging from the conflictual flux of images of phallic grandeur and depletion, rivalrous triumph and defeat, threats to genital intactness, and envy of the penis or womb. From the standpoint of the articulation and consolidation of the self representation, the successful passing of the oedipal period crystallizes the rudiments of an enduring gender identity, gender-specific ambitions and ideals, and an awareness of gender-specific strengths, capacities, vulnerabilities, and limitations (Ross, 1977).

The occurrence of phallic and oedipal imagery signals in turn the achievement of further developmental steps. Penis and womb envy indicate that recognition of sexual differences has been established. Castration or penetration anxiety reflect a newly acquired but precarious consolidation of both a sense of bodily intactness and a sexually differentiated body image. Finally, oedipal imagery attests to the growing tolerance for ambivalent feelings and the capacity for maintaining complex triadic relationships with constant objects.

To summarize, the psychosexual experiences, fantasies, and enactments that occur in the course of normal development may be viewed both as *psychic organizers* (Spitz, 1959) which contribute significantly to the structuralization of the representational world and of the self representation in particular, and as indicators of developmental steps in the consolidation of self and object representations. Nature, in her evolutionary wisdom, has harnessed the exquisiteness of sensual pleasure to serve the ontogenesis of subjectivity. This conception of the vital developmental importance of psychosexual experience helps us to understand the extremely damaging effects that traumatic overstimulations, deprivations, and other early distortions in the sphere of sensual experience can have in interfering with the normal consolidation of self and object representations. An appreciation of the role of psychosexuality in normal representational development also sheds light on the meaning of adult sexual pathology, particularly in developmentally arrested patients.

THE REPRESENTATIONAL WORLD IN SEXUAL PERVERSIONS

In normal development, psychosexual experiences contribute crucially to the articulation and consolidation of self and object representations. When perverse sexual fantasies and acts occur in developmentally arrested individuals, in whom self and object representations are insufficiently structuralized, this function of early psychosexual experience may be revived in order to shore up a precarious and imperiled representational world. In such cases, it is not, contrary to what Freud (1905b) maintained, the erotic experience per se that has been fixated and then regressively reanimated; instead, it is the early infantile *function* of the erotic experience that is retained and regressively relied upon—its function in maintaining the structural cohesion and stability of crumbling, fragmenting, disintegrating self and object representations.

This is not to say that structure maintenance is the only aim of perverse sexual fantasy and activity. Like any complex psychological product, sexual perversions are multiply determined and serve multiple functions (Waelder, 1936; Brenman, 1952; Lachmann, 1975), the motivational importance of which will vary from one patient to another. For neurotically organized patients, perversion may function principally as a regressive defense against oedipal conflicts and reassurance against the threat of castration (Freud, 1927; Fenichel, 1945) or as a hostile, vindictive triumph over traumatogenic early

object imagoes (Stoller, 1975). However, for structurally
deficient, developmentally arrested patients, the moti-
vationally most urgent function of perverse activity is
likely to pertain to an impelling need to restore or maintain the intactness of self and object representations
which are threatened with dissolution.

A number of analysts have contributed important insights into the function of sexual perversions in shoring
up precarious representational structures. According to
Socarides (1973, 1974, 1978, 1979), for example, perversion is the product of an inability to pass successfully
through the symbiotic and separation-individuation phases
of early childhood, a developmental failure which results
in severe deficits in ego functioning. Perversion, in turn,
serves the repression of the urge to regress to a preoedipal
fixation in which there is a desire for and dread of merging with the mother in order to reinstate the primitive,
undifferentiated mother-child unity. By implication, the
function of sexual perversion is, in part, to compensate
for a structural impairment in self-object boundaries, a
remnant of a developmental arrest.

The function of pathological sexual activity in resti-
tuting or maintaining the fragile self representations of
narcissistically disturbed patients has been systematically elucidated by Kohut (1971, 1977; see also A. Reich,
1960; Goldberg, 1975). Kohut has demonstrated that a
wide variety of perverse activities may be viewed as primitively sexualized attempts to compensate for voids and
defects in the structure of the self and to counteract experiences of inner deadness and self-fragmentation. In
the perverse act, the patient sexualizes an archaic narcissistic configuration in an effort to find an eroticized
replacement for the selfobjects who in his formative years
were traumatically absent, disappointing, or unresponsive to his developmental requirements, a sequence of

events which may be repeated in the course of analysis whenever the patient experiences a narcissistic injury or disruption in the narcissistic transference.

In chapter 3 we examined the narcissistic function of masochism, including masochistic perversion. We proposed that in structurally deficient, developmentally arrested patients, masochistic experiences might serve to restore or sustain the cohesion and stability of a damaged, menaced, or disintegrating self representation through the stimulations afforded by pain and skin eroticism, through exhibitionistic displays of suffering to a real or imaginary audience, through mergings with omnipotent object imagoes, and by creating a fantasied identity between the actual self and the primitive grandiose self. Extrapolating from the ideas of Nydes (1950) and Eissler (1958) on the power of the orgasm to create and confirm conviction, it was suggested that the experience of orgasm in the sadomasochistic perversions (and other perversions as well) might serve to revitalize ecstatically the structurally deficient individual's sense of conviction about the truth and reality of his having a bounded and cohesive self. Furthermore, the degree of primitive sexualization, as well as aggressivization, of narcissistic reparative efforts is a measure of the degree of narcissistic vulnerability and the acuteness of the threat of narcissistic decompensation. The Janus-faced quality of the orgasm in both offering the promise of self-articulation and posing the threat of self-dissolution might account for the elaborate ritualization with which the structurally deficient person must surround his perverse acts.

Clinical material follows to illustrate the reciprocal relationship between perverse sexual fantasies and acts and self and object representations in varying degrees of consolidation. Analytic exploration of rape fantasies and homosexual exhibitionistic enactments, their origins and functions, revealed the particular ways in which they compensated for specific structural weaknesses or averted specific threats to the integrity, continuity, and affective tone of self and object representations. The appearance of penis envy, on the other hand, was seen to signal newly acquired representational structure.

RAPE FANTASIES AND PENIS ENVY

Sandra began her six-year analysis at age 25 because feelings of anxiety, shame, and humiliation, along with fears of having these feelings, inhibited her work as an actress. She suffered from considerable performance anxiety which affected her ability to control her voice. Both of her parents had relinquished their own acting aspirations in order to support their family and were now involved in neighborhood amateur theaters. Sandra's anxieties appeared when she was about to make the transition from "gifted" amateur to competitive professional.

Though Sandra's father had achieved prominence in his business, he was clearly subjugated by her mother in the home. According to Sandra, her younger brother played a minor role in the family and she barely mentioned him during the early years of the analysis.

Sandra was groomed by her mother to be a performer from the age of five on. Her mother coached her, pushed her, and applauded her until Sandra's talents clearly enabled her to make her own way. At that point the mother-daughter relationship became severely strained. During the earlier, formative years, conflicts between mother and daughter rarely surfaced, with Sandra habitually complying with her mother's expectations and values. In turn, Sandra's image of herself as perfect, good, pure, unambitious, and uncompetitive was supported, and a mergerlike tie to her mother was perpetuated.

Viewed from the standpoint of psychosexual development, Sandra's stage fright could be seen as a displace-
ment from an anal-phase struggle. One line of associations
during the analysis led to the understanding that to be
observed performing meant to be observed on the toilet.
The conflict over who controlled the content of her
body—what she produced through her bowels or her
voice—had clearly been resolved in favor of her mother's
supremacy. From the standpoint of the structuralization
of Sandra's representational world, a firm differentiation
between the self and maternal object representation was
impeded. Her sense of self-esteem became grounded in
a pattern of compliance and submission which maintained the mergerlike bond with her mother as an archaic
selfobject and sustained the image of herself as her
mother's pure and innocent young girl.

Interpretations of Sandra's defenses against aggression toward her mother evoked unbearable anxiety. It
became apparent that such interpretations produced an
intolerable dilemma in which she felt pressured to separate from her mother at a time when her self representation was not sufficiently differentiated or structured.
Pursuing this line of interpretation further would have
created within the analysis a repetition of the traumatic
anal struggle which had already brought her productiv-
ity to a halt.

Rather than implicitly encouraging the expression of
aggression toward her mother as a way of fostering separation, the analytic work focused on the recognition and
verbalization of her need to feel merged with her mother
as a source of power, magical protection, and self-esteem,
and her need to avoid experiences of separation. She was
then able to express fears that she could become a helpless victim of her mother's envy and retaliation. Exploration of the power and control attributed to her mother

unveiled her unconscious fantasy of a phallic mother.

In the course of the analysis Sandra became professionally more successful and was able to acknowledge the satisfaction she derived from both her work and the applause of her audiences. In turn, her tie with her mother and the required image of herself as unambitious, unaggressive, and uncompetitive—i.e., as pure and innocent—were increasingly placed in jeopardy. Conscious fantasies during sexual intercourse of being raped and degraded, which had appeared sporadically in the past, now became more frequent, occurring typically in connection with successes or the anticipation of a successful performance. For Sandra, the meaning of the rape fantasies was *not* predominantly that of defensively reversing a potentially "aggressive" act. Primarily they served a narcissistic function by restoring a positively toned self representation. The "rapist" in these fantasies was derived from the image of the phallic mother. The fantasies revitalized this image and averted separation by enabling Sandra, once again, to feel controlled by and merged with the powerful maternal object. Hence, through these fantasies Sandra reinstated the image of herself as her mother's pure and innocent young girl, an image that she still required for her self-esteem.

After this material was partially worked through, Sandra produced dreams in which she possessed a penis. These dreams could have been interpreted as a defensive identification with the aggressor, i.e., with the phallic mother, but from the standpoint of the differentiation and consolidation of her self representation another line of interpretation seemed germane. The dreams were interpreted as reflecting the attainment of a developmental step. She could now imagine herself as powerful and less vulnerable. Her vulnerability to regressive mergers had passed. The dreams suggested that her mother had been demoted from the position of power and supremacy that she had once occupied. At this point, for Sandra to have a penis meant that her mother did not have it. The imagery was interpreted as signaling that a degree of self-object separation had been attained, a developmental advance beyond Sandra's earlier states of merger with the powerful and controlling maternal object (cf. the case of Miss V, Kohut, 1977).

Working through the fantasy of possessing a penis ushered in a period of homosexual fantasy with some homosexual activity. The actual homosexual experience was "marred" for Sandra by her constant awareness that she lacked a penis. In turn, her feelings of disappointment led to the emergence of intense, pervasive penis envy. While the envy was open to various interpretations, in terms of the development of her representational world, the emphasis was placed on her painful recognition and acceptance of genital differences and her integration of a gender-specific limitation (i.e., the lack of a penis) into her self representation. In short, her self and object representations were becoming more realistic and less vulnerable to regressions.

For Sandra, the progression from rape fantasies to penis envy signaled a developmental step in the structuralization of her representational world—in the articulation and differentiation of self and object images and the consolidation of self-object boundaries. Specifically, it indicated a firming of a body image which included genital features—albeit to her regret. In the imagery which accompanied her envy (at first, fantasies of men dominating women with their penises; later, ideas about various male prerogatives) Sandra acknowledged genital differences and placed the penis on the man, with the painful realization that both she and her mother lacked one. This heralded a firming of her gender identity and a definitive shift toward heterosexuality, i.e., toward her father as her principal love object. As her self representation gradually became more consolidated, Sandra was able to relinquish her mother as an archaic selfobject and establish a more or less realistic relationship with her. Concurrently her brother was brought out from the shadows of her memory. She was able to recall her early intense competition with him and triumphs over him and, for the first time, to establish a friendship with him.

Recognition and acknowledgement of the developmental significance of Sandra's penis envy was pivotal for the progress of her treatment. Had the analyst interpreted the penis envy as merely reflecting pathological fixations and defenses, the patient's developmental thrusts toward greater self-object separation would most probably have been aborted, as they had been in her early "anal" struggles with her mother. By understanding and interpreting the significance of the envy as a developmental indicator, issuing from advances in the structuralization of the patient's self and object representations, the analyst was able to facilitate the further evolution and consolidation of her representational world.

In contrast to Sandra, rape fantasies served another patient primarily as a defense warding off memories of primal-scene observations. Joan, a 28-year-old single woman, knew that she had slept in her parents' bedroom until the age of eleven, but she had no conscious recollections of this. Her repression of primal-scene images was aided by the establishment of a defensive self representation as "unaware." In turn, this interfered with learning, which became unconsciously equated with acquiring sexual knowledge. Reading sometimes resulted in unbearable excitement and anxiety because, by threatening to "enlighten" her, it collided with her defensive need to remain "unaware."

Joan's rape fantasies permitted her to engage in sexual activity while preserving her image of herself as the
sleeper who saw nothing in her parents' bedroom and
who was only now being aroused from her innocence. The
rape fantasies occurred in two forms: they appeared
overtly in daydreams accompanying sexual relations and
they covertly structured her experience in various non-
sexual situations. In these latter situations, she continually needed to evaluate who was the "rapist" and who
was "raped." For example, in conducting her interior dec-
orating business, it was necessary for her to make in-
quiries of dealers, which made her feel "too intrusive"
and "dominating" and threatened to place her in the position usually occupied by the rapist in her fantasies. Her
frequent "forgetting" to make various business calls resulted from her need to reaffirm her defensive self representation as "unaware."

The rape fantasies entertained by Sandra and Joan
had different origins and meanings. Sandra's image of
herself as pure and innocent, while embodying reaction
formations against anality, grew primarily from her need
to maintain a mergerlike attachment to her mother as
her principal source of self-esteem regulation. This self
representation was incompletely demarcated from the
maternal object and hence was endangered by experiences of separation. Rape fantasies permitted sexual
pleasure while simultaneously affirming her mother's
greater power and superiority. Primarily, however, they
served to restore a positively toned self representation
when experiences of separation from her mother menaced
the mergerlike bond that was essential for her self-esteem.

Joan's self representation as unaware grew out of her
defensive need to keep primal-scene material repressed.
Rape fantasies buttressed this repression by reassuring

her that she had been sexually ignorant and that sexual knowledge was only now being forced upon her.

Sandra's rapist was essentially the "phallic" mother, while Joan's was the oedipal father. Thus the emergence of material reflecting penis envy had different implications in their treatment. Sandra's penis envy signaled a developmental step in the articulation and differentiation of self and object images and the consolidation of self-object boundaries. Joan's penis envy served a defensive function in warding off oedipally tinged sexual fantasies. Joan's representational world was firmly structured, but was pervaded by highly conflictual sexual images and meanings derived from the excessive sexual stimulations during her formative years.

Finally, the significance of sexual orgasms differed for the two patients. Joan avoided the experience of orgasm during intercourse because it would have jeopardized her defensive self representation as "unaware." Sandra's orgasms during intercourse affirmed the accompanying fantasies and hence lent a sense of conviction to her narcissistic restorative efforts. At first, orgasms were possible for Sandra because they helped to create an illusion of merging with the phallic mother. Eventually they became incorporated into a more differentiated, heterosexual self representation.

HOMOSEXUAL EXHIBITIONISM

The reciprocal relation between impairment in self-object differentiation and sexual pathology can be seen clearly in the contrasting cases of homosexuality described by Kohut (1971) and Socarides (1969). Both described patients whose homosexuality was based on preoedipal disturbances. Socarides, however, emphasized the defensive aspects of the homosexuality. His patient was dominated by an image of a sadistic preoedipal mother who might kill or engulf him and thus obliterate his personal identity. The homosexuality thus protected him against engulfment and the self-dissolution that he feared would accompany attempts at separation from the preoedipal mother. While these fears could be seen to reflect insufficiently consolidated self and object representations, Socarides stressed the defensive purposes of the homosexuality. Kohut's patient embarked upon homosexual (voyeuristic) activities to avert the threat to his self representation brought on by even brief separations from his analyst. Primarily the patient attempted to compensate for the missing part of his self structure, as personified by the missing analyst, by gazing at men in public toilets and achieving a feeling of merger with them (Kohut, 1971). Warding off an anticipated intrapsychic danger was not the principal meaning of the homosexual preoccupation. Rather, it reflected an attempt to reestablish a sense of self-cohesion.

We turn now to a homosexual perversion in which the sexual fantasies and enactments served to repair and sustain an insufficiently structured self representation. Mark was 35 years old when he sought treatment because he felt he was "not getting anywhere" professionally. He thought that for a person of his intelligence he should be earning more than he did as a middle-level executive in a public relations firm. He attributed his general feeling of unhappiness to his advancing age and to the hectic quality of big-city life. He believed he had little in common with his co-workers and felt socially isolated in his job. Feelings of isolation and estrangment were also characteristic of his childhood years. As a child, he preferred drawing houses and architectural designs in his home to playing with his schoolmates on the sports field. In his college years, his good looks, charm, and good manners gained him admission to the country club set and thus enabled him to rise above his economically modest origins. Dating girls was in the service of social climbing and status seeking. He became seriously interested in a girl in his class after noticing the label from a prestigious store in her coat. Homosexuality was sporadic during his college years, and he became exclusively homosexual after graduating. Three years before Mark began treatment, his father, an alcoholic, committed suicide. His mother was still alive, and Mark had remained, since childhood, her confidant and admirer.

The narcissistic transference that evolved in treatment revived Mark's archaic grandiose self and his need for the analyst to function as an admiring mirror. Early in treatment he described having a conversation with the president of his firm, who later had asked Mark's immediate supervisor about the "snotty" man to whom he had just spoken. When Mark was told of this he was surprised, for he thought he had behaved well, had spoken politely, and had acted in a conciliatory manner. While recounting these events, a strange expression came over Mark's face and, when asked about it, he responded: "Oh, my mother used to point that out to me when I was a child. She called it a superior smile."

Analytic exploration of the meaning of the smile and the reasons it emerged as it did led to the interpretation of a conflict, quite superficially conceptualized, between Mark's intention to behave in an obliging manner toward the president and his urge to disassociate himself from him because Mark secretly viewed him with contempt. This material emerged as a result of the first joint exploration in the treatment, a temporary shift in the therapeutic relationship which was only later understood as a disruption of the narcissistic mirror transference.

The effect of this exploration was to evoke consider-

able anxiety, producing sleep disturbances and nightmares in which two cars crashed headlong into each
other. Viewed from the standpoint of the patient's narcissistic requirements, being called "snotty" by the president depleted his grandiose self and having the smile
brought to his attention by the analyst revived a similar
and earlier blow to his grandiosity inflicted by his
mother. His mother criticized the smile and hoped to
eliminate it by drawing his attention to it. The analytic
intervention had a similar depleting impact by failing
to take into account the narcissistic function of the
smile—it had served to restore an image of himself as
"superior" in the context of having failed to receive the
requisite admiration. Hence, confronting Mark in this
manner with his smile threatened the integrity of his
self representation.

Mark's anxiety and dream of the crashing cars can be
seen as reflecting his fear of the dissolution of his grandiose self under the impact of the analyst's empathic failure and deficient mirroring. Certain associations to the
cars led to memories of the importance of cars for restitutive, exhibitionistic purposes for both Mark and his
father. Furthermore, the patient and his homosexual
lover had recently jointly purchased a car. Other associations revealed that sometime during late adolescence
Mark had gone on a drunken joyride that resulted in a
crash in which he suffered many lacerations, especially
on his face. Thus, the crashing cars in the dream alluded
to a shattering deflation of his exhibitionistic strivings,
and the car as a symbol encompassed both his exhibitionistic and reparative efforts and his fear of the destruction of his grandiose self.

Recognition of the self-restorative function of the
smile enabled Mark to recover memories of severe sham-
ings and humiliations inflicted by his mother when he

failed to meet the stringent and phase-inappropriate standards of manner and dress that she imposed. An emerging theme was his mother's undermining of his phase-appropriate phallic exhibitionism and independent grandiose strivings and Mark's assumption of the role of his mother's admiring confidant and narcissistic extension. In the position of "restrained" parent to his mother, a "little gentleman" wise beyond his years, he could preserve a precarious grandiosity to which his "superior" smile eventually became heir.

Mark brought dreams to the sessions, the associations to which led to the recovery of repressed memories. A dream image of a little child who sat on the shoulders of an adult and urinated on him first led Mark to mention that he had recently forgotten to plug up the drain of the swimming pool in his summer house so that a neighbor's lawn was flooded. In turn, this enabled him to recall the searing humiliation he felt when, at age three, he "embarrassed" his mother by urinating on the floor. Finally, he recovered further memories from his early teens in which he urinated on the kitchen floor in order to roll around on his urine.

The analyst postponed the interpretation of the aggressive wishes conveyed in the dream imagery for later phases of the treatment. He focused instead on the vulnerability of Mark's self representation and in particular on his need to shore up the intactness of his precarious body boundaries by creating from his own body fluids a replacement for the warm, affirming sensual contact that his object world was failing to provide. Mark then recovered memories in which his heretofore "perfect" and idealized mother had been grossly unempathic. For example, he recalled winning an award in high school and his feelings of deep hurt and disappointment when his mother became "bored" during the ceremony and left the auditorium before he was awarded his prize. His mother gradually emerged in his memories as a vain, self-engrossed woman who possessed little ability to provide Mark with either the warm, sensual body contact or the narcissistic confirmations which are prerequisites for the consolidation of a cohesive and stable body image.

The evolution of Mark's homosexual perversion and its function of restoring and sustaining a precarious self representation can be reconstructed, beginning with the shame-filled urination memory from age three. This memory telescoped both earlier and later experiences of self-fragmentation in which his grandiosity was depleted and his self image suffused with shame through traumatic rebuffs of his phase-appropriate exhibitionism. Self-restoration by rolling in his own urine was later replaced with masturbation in front of a mirror in which he imagined the sight of a perfect version of himself, whereupon he could feel for the moment transformed into an imaginary picture of physical perfection. The self-reparative and self-restitutive functions of these earlier practices acquired a definitive, enduring sexualization in the homosexuality which germinated during his later college years. The preferred form of homosexual activity that finally emerged involved sexual acts performed exhibitionistically in a public homosexual setting where he could feel enhanced by the admiration of his onlookers.

Mark felt no conscious ambivalence about his homosexuality, only distress over his social isolation and his increasing failure to receive the admiration he required for his sense of self. He sought immersion in homosexual exhibitionistic activities so that he could feel reassured by the gleam reflected back to him by his audience. At the same time, he sought union with an admiring, idealized, sexually identical partner who simultaneously confirmed and duplicated Mark's own grandiose-perfectionistic self. In their mirror functions, his audience and his partner were heirs to the urine and to the literal mirror of his earlier pubertal years. Through them, he sought to reinstate and preserve an image of himself as physically intact and perfect, attractive and never boring, and ultimately invulnerable to the "slings and arrows" emanating from the object world.

Mark's self-restitutive attempts could not keep pace with the increasing severity of blows to his self-esteem. Both aging and the widening gap between his grandiose self-expectations and what to him were modest successes required ever increasing efforts to bolster self-esteem. Thus he veered more and more toward seeking in sexual and social relationships the admiration and restorative gleam he so desperately needed. His underlying motive for seeking treatment was his wish to become a more perfect version of what he already believed himself to be. The self-centeredness of his demands had resulted in ever greater social ostracism, which had become increasingly difficult for him to rationalize. Under the pressure of continual narcissistic injuries, he revived archaic forms of erotic stimulation in an effort to restore the affective tone, continuity, and cohesion of his precarious self representation. For Mark, the experience of sexual orgasm lent a feeling of conviction and reality to the illusory perfection and to the sense of self-cohesion which the exhibitionistic enactments provided.

TREATMENT IMPLICATIONS

Having in previous chapters described in detail the analytic interpretation of developmentally arrested self and object representations, we now wish to consider two related issues—the analytic approach to aggression and acting out.

The Analytic Approach to Aggression

In distinguishing between idealizations and grandiosity rooted in developmental arrests and those which reflect intrapsychic conflict, we have suggested that the arousal of aggression can enhance self-object differentiation and call the narcissistic configurations into the service of defense. In the treatment of narcissistic pathology arising from intrapsychic conflicts (Kernberg, 1975), defenses against aggression can be systematically analyzed.

With those patients in whom aggressive affects and wishes were not sufficient to aid in the development of self-object separation, and for whom aggression would now pose a serious threat to a vitally needed tie to a selfobject (see the case of Jane, ch. 5), the analyst must proceed with caution. To promote the emergence of hostility while the self representation is still insufficiently structured, vulnerable, and in need of selfobjects for the maintenance of its cohesion and stability places the patient in an intolerable dilemma. In effect, the patient is encouraged to bite the hand that sustains him.

A case reported by the research study group of The Psychoanalytic Research and Development Fund (Ostow, 1974) touches on a similar point. The patient suffered from intense anxiety because he could not live up to the brilliance expected of him. His previous analyst, whom he described as "almost a god," had urged him to express his rage toward his mother for being the cause of his ruination. This, he was told, would set him free. The patient obeyed, but immediately thereafter began his first homosexual encounter. Homosexuality, for this patient, served to re-establish a self representation as "powerful . . . potent and manly" (Ostow, 1974, p. 91) when his tie to his mother as an archaic selfobject became endangered.

In the treatment of Sandra, interpretations of her need for her mother as a selfobject and of her developmental steps in self-object differentiation as reflected in shifts in her psychosexual imagery preceded the emergence of competitive themes and hostile feelings toward her mother. The steps through which the self representation became increasingly articulated and structuralized finally led to her greater tolerance of aggressive wishes and feelings toward objects, as signaled by the appearance of fantasies of possessing a penis and of penis envy.

A sensitive point in Sandra's treatment was the interpretation of her attachment to her mother's fantasied magical protection. Sandra saw this as a "suggestion" to "separate" from her mother by not speaking to her—that is, by withholding her vocal products. Had the analyst pursued further her fear of expressing aggression to her mother or mother surrogates or focused on her inability to assert herself, Sandra would have experienced it as a demand that she relinquish her tie to her mother as an archaic selfobject. It would have required that she take this step without as yet having developed a firmly differentiated and structured self representation. Instead, the analytic exploration focused on understanding her need for her mother and the vital functions served by the archaic tie. As her self representation gradually consolidated in concert with psychosexual fantasies signaling increasing articulation of her representational world, she was able to relinquish her mother as an archaic selfobject and establish a more or less realistic relationship with her.

Mark's aggression had not been sufficiently harnessed in the service of intrapsychic separation, and his continued need for selfobjects became manifest in the analytic situation as a mirror transference. When rage at selfobjects was aroused reactively by blows to his grandiose self, he experienced an alarming loss of self-cohesion and a dramatic collapse in his self-esteem. Thus, for Mark too, the analysis of aggression required special tact. In developmentally arrested patients, premature arousal of reactive aggression can have the effect of promoting narcissistic withdrawal and sexualized compensatory activities, rather than promoting intrapsychic separation, assertiveness, and ambivalence tolerance.

The Analytic Approach to Acting Out

Mark experienced the analytic exploration of his smile as a painful confrontation and momentary rupture in the mirror transference. His anxiety and sleep disturbances reflected the temporary fragmentation of his precarious grandiose self. However, exploring the meaning of the smile also elicited Mark's curiosity and some capacity for self-observation. His associations led him to understand the sense of security he gained in seeing himself as an unprovocative person. The smile, however, conveyed contempt, and it was upsetting to him to discover that he had exposed this provocative attitude. As this was spelled out, his anxiety diminished. Then, after feeling better for a few weeks, he indicated that he wanted to take a three-month "vacation" from treatment to "think over" what he had learned. The analyst responded that, while Mark might use the "vacation" in a way that could be useful to him, it might also represent a flight which could slow down his treatment. Mark replied that he was fully aware of these possibilities, but that he wished to try it on his own anyway. And so, after about six months of treatment he left, but three months later, almost to the day, he called to resume analysis. It was then, after the vacation, that the major portion of the analytic work took place.

By accepting Mark's vacation as a potentially con-

structive step, rather than interpreting it solely as a resistive act or "acting out" and focusing immediately on
what he was attempting to ward off, the analyst enabled
him to return to treatment with the budding narcissistic
transference unharmed. Later, Mark was able to explore
the meanings of the act.

Mark's wish to take the vacation was provoked unwittingly when the analyst pointed out his smile, prematurely depleting his grandiose self. Because a
therapeutic alliance was not present at the beginning of
the treatment, Mark's continual need for mirroring and
admiration of his grandiose self left little room for tactful
confrontations or joint explorations. However, after the
vacation, his communications became less guarded, and
he began to provide descriptions of the painful, shame-
ridden experiences of his childhood. The mirror transference was still very much in evidence, but a rudimentary therapeutic alliance was beginning to take root, so
that joint exploration of material became an increasing
possibility.

The vacation was a crucial event in the treatment. In
looking back upon it later in treatment, it was understood
to have been partly a test to determine whether the analyst would allow Mark to separate or would hold on to
him for his own personal needs, as his mother had. Additionally, Mark took the vacation because he needed this
concrete act—just as he needed concrete sexual enactments—since verbalization and fantasy alone would not
have sufficed to provide the requisite narcissistic restoration. In retrospect, the potential danger to the treatment lay not so much in the exploration of the smile as
in the handling of the vacation. The analyst's nonjudgmental acceptance of the vacation enabled the patient to
return, having enacted a developmental step whereby
the analyst could then, on occasion, be accepted as a separate object.

SUMMARY AND CONCLUSIONS

We have explored the reciprocal relation between sexual fantasy and activity and the development of self and object representations. The various phases of psychosexual organization contribute not only to the content of self and object images but also to their differentiation and integration. Thus, the sensual experiences, fantasies, and enactments that occur in the course of normal development are seen as psychic organizers which contribute vitally to the structuralization of the representational world. In the perverse sexual fantasies and acts which occur in developmentally arrested individuals, this function of early psychosexual experiences has been retained and is regressively relied upon when self and object representations are endangered.

We presented two clinical cases to illustrate the differing origins and meanings of rape fantasies. For Sandra, these were remnants of a developmental arrest and served to restore vulnerable self and object images. Penis envy occurred as a developmental advance indicating that self and object representations had become more firmly structuralized. In contrast, for Joan both rape fantasies and penis envy served to ward off primal-scene memories in the context of structural conflict.

The case of Mark illustrated the narcissistic function of perverse sexual activity (homosexual exhibitionism) in restoring and sustaining a precarious self representation. Both sexual fantasy and perverse activity can serve to repair or maintain insufficiently structured (developmentally arrested) self and object images, and viewed from that vantage point important treatment implications follow. Our thesis that, in the case of psychopathology rooted in developmental arrests, the analyst interprets the selfobject configurations that the patient is attempting to maintain or achieve, has been further elaborated with respect to the analytic approach to aggression and acting out.

In cases of structural conflict, the analysis of the defenses against aggressive affects and wishes aids in the resolution of conflict and furthers the articulation of self and object images. In cases of psychopathology rooted in insufficiently structured self and object representations, such a focus may be experienced as premature pressure to separate and thus provoke regression. In contrast, the analyst's empathic clarifications of the patient's specific need for archaic selfobjects promotes differentiation and structuralization. In a similar vein, a "vacation" from treatment, usually understood in the analysis of structural conflict as "acting out" or resistive, can, in the analysis of developmental arrests, be understood as a concrete enactment which is required for the protection of imperiled representational structures or for the establishment of a specific selfobject bond.

9

Developmental Arrests and the Psychoanalytic Situation

We have seen that the extension of psychoanalytic practice beyond the classical psychoneuroses to the treatment of severe characterological, narcissistic, borderline, and psychotic disorders has made it necessary to distinguish between psychopathology that is the product of intrapsychic conflicts and psychopathology that is the remnant of developmental voids, deficits, and arrests. This vital theoretical distinction, central to this book, illuminates a diverse array of clinical phenomena: narcissism; masochism and sadism; denial fantasies; idealization and grandiosity; projection, incorporation, and splitting; death anxiety, hypochrondriasis, and depersonalization; and sexual fantasy and perverse activity. In this concluding chapter we expand upon the implications of our theoretical ideas and clinical findings for conceptualizing the psychoanalytic situation and its therapeutic action in the treatment of developmental arrests.

SUMMARY OF THEORETICAL CONTRIBUTIONS

Four general theoretical conclusions can be drawn from our work:

171

First, the developmental lines leading to the differentiation, integration, and consolidation of self and object representations are of critical importance in conceptualizing the more severe forms of psychopathology and their treatment. An understanding of the origins and consequences of interferences with and arrests in this developmental progression provides a broader and more embracing view of psychopathology and therapy than was possible within the framework of classical conflict theory. Furthermore, a theoretical comprehension of developmental deficits and arrests has crucial implications for the precise framing of analytic interventions and for conceptualizing the course and therapeutic action of psychoanalytic treatment.

Second, in order to be able to understand and treat structurally deficient, developmentally arrested patients, the principle of multiple function (Waelder, 1936) must be expanded to include a consideration of the ways in which the varieties of psychopathology function to restore or maintain precarious or imperiled self and object representations which, in the course of development, have not been adequately consolidated. The motivational priority or urgency of this latter function, as well as the degree of its primitive sexualization or aggressivization, will vary according to the severity of structural impairment and the acuteness of the threat of structural decompensation. This conceptualization is particularly important for the understanding and therapeutic approach to the primitive, perverse, sadomasochistic, and exhibitionistic fantasies and acts of developmentally arrested patients.

Third, the concept of defense must be reformulated within a developmental framework. There is a developmental line for each defensive process, with precursors or prestages of the defenses occurring prior to the structuralization of self and object representations. Hence, a defense in the usual sense of the term represents the endpoint of a series of developmental achievements. We cannot assume that all patients have accomplished these developmental steps.

Fourth, it is of utmost theoretical and therapeutic importance to distinguish between mental activity that functions principally as a defense, warding off components of intrapsychic conflicts, and superficially similar mental activity that is more accurately understood as a remnant of an arrest at a prestage of defensive development characterized by deficiencies in the consolidation of self and object representations. This distinction, with its important technical implications, makes possible the recognition of the ways in which a variety of psychological products may not only express psychopathology but also signal the attainment of developmental steps in the structuralization of the representational world.

ANALYTIC INTERVENTIONS

We now turn to an exploration of the technical and therapeutic implications of our theoretical conclusions. Our focus is on the degree of self-object differentiation and representational integration discernible in pathological constellations and on the extent to which cohesive and stable self and object representations have been established and consolidated.

The crucial diagnostic distinction the analyst must make at any given point in the treatment is between a classical transference phenomenon in which he is primarily experienced as a separate, more or less differentiated and integrated whole object—a target of displaced affects and conflictual wishes—and a primitive representational configuration in which he is predominantly experienced as an archaic, prestructural selfobject. An important aspect of this ongoing diagnostic assessment is an evaluation as to whether defensive processes or developmentally arrested prestages of defenses predominate in the patient's psychopathology. The therapeutic relationship may shift back and forth between the more advanced and more primitive positions throughout the analysis. These progressive and regressive shifts occur as the patient's psychopathology unfolds and is met with the required empathy and skillful interpretations. The two levels of object relationship may coexist. A communication to the analyst may at one point in the treatment require that he respond from the position of an archaic selfobject and at another point, to similar material, from the position of a separate and whole object. A careful assessment of the motivational priority or urgency of the multiple functions served by a psychological configuration will directly determine the content and timing of interpretations.

When the analyst becomes established for the patient as an archaic selfobject, the maintenance of this primitive state is necessary for the gradual differentiation, integration, and consolidation of self and object representations. The protection of this primitive representational configuration against traumatic disruptions requires of the analyst that he recognize and clarify the patient's specific vulnerabilities and restitutive strivings. The treatment of Jane, Sandra, Mark, Mary, and James exemplified this therapeutic principle. The treatment of these patients can be contrasted with others in whom there were surface similarities to patients with developmental arrests. However, careful evaluation of the transference relationships formed by the patients in this second group revealed that the analyst was a separate and whole object for them—richly experienced and the target of complex, conflictual wishes and displaced affects. This group includes patients like Anna, Rachel, and Joan. In their treatment, interpretations of sexual and aggressive wishes and defenses against them were required. The case of Reginald stands between the two positions just described. Though a narcissistic transference was established, this was understood as a *regressive defense* against intrapsychic conflict, rather than as a *regressive revival of a developmental arrest.* As with Anna, Rachel, and Joan, with Reginald the therapeutic task required the interpretation of the conflicts he was warding off rather than states he was attempting to maintain or achieve.

A fourth group of patients are those in whom self and object representations are insufficiently structured and, in addition, whose capacities for representational differentiation and synthesis are so severely impaired that they require supplementation by specific interventions from the analyst. In the treatment of these patients, the analyst must provide a model for the defective discriminative and integrative functions by articulating for the patient these usually silent processes. In the treatment of Bill, Burton, and the patient described by Atkin (1975), interventions were addressed to the patient's need for the analyst to aid in demonstrating the distinction between self and object and to provide a model for synthesizing constrasting self and object representations.

In cases of developmental arrest, careful assessment of the quality of the therapeutic relationship enables the analyst to adopt a therapeutic stance which gradually promotes the structuralization of precarious self and object representations. Specifically, the analyst will consistently convey his empathic understanding of the developmental significance of the primitive states or representational structures the patient needs to maintain or achieve. Examples of such states include the restoration of a symbioticlike merger which had been precipitously or phase-inappropriately disrupted, the reliance upon archaic selfobject configurations to sustain a vulnerable self representation, or the use of a model to aid in the demarcation and synthesis of inadequately structured self and object representations.

In the treatment of developmental arrests, reconstructions of the patient's past alert the analyst to pathogenic developmental traumata which he will strive not to repeat with the patient. Genetic reconstructions will also help the analyst to understand the patient's reactions to the inevitable unwitting repetitions that do occur and to comprehend the missed or prematurely lost developmental phases and aborted developmental thrusts that the patient needs to resume within the therapeutic relationship.

The analyst's correct assessment and empathic interpretive responses permit the arrested representational configurations to emerge and evolve. Signals of this developmental process, because of their surface similarity to frequently encountered resistive transference manifestations found in cases of conflict pathology, may be misunderstood and incorrectly interpreted with a view toward defense analysis. Such signals of representational development may include a greater tolerance of aggressive affect and increasing self-assertiveness, including oppositional behavior, on the part of the patient, as well as attempts to induce the analyst to assert his existence as a separate object or to adopt a critical or antagonistic stance (as in the case of Jane). The appearance of certain symptoms (such as death anxiety, hypochondriasis, and depersonalization), of specific psychosexual imagery (such as castration anxiety and penis envy), and of episodes of sexual and aggressive acting out may also at times signal a newly acquired and thus fragile consolidation of self and object representations (Bill, Mary, Sandra, and Mark). At the very least, the analyst must take care that erroneous defense interpretations do not discourage the emerging structuralization. At most, an empathic confirmation from the analyst may be required.

In a similar vein, varying internalizations of the analyst ranging from primitive, global imitations to subtle, partial identifications must be evaluated in terms of the existing object relationship with the analyst to determine the extent to which these internalizations serve defensive purposes and the extent to which they signal the beginnings of structure acquisition, whereby self and object representations acquire greater cohesion and stability.

Particularly during the early phases of treatment, the analyst needs to be alert to the role of arrested developmental aspects of the psychopathology, since errors in the direction of interpreting remnants of developmental arrests as products of intrapsychic conflicts are more damaging for the treatment than errors in the reverse direction. Furthermore, a correct approach to the arrested developmental aspects during the early stages of treatment may be required in order to help the patient acquire the psychological structure which is a prerequisite for the subsequent working through of intrapsychic conflicts and the defenses against them. The achievement of a requisite degree of consolidation of self and object representations is especially important for the working through of conflicts over aggression. Our cases illustrate that, when structuralization of the representational world has reached a level required for the working through of such conflicts, the patient will signal this readiness to the analyst.

THE PSYCHOANALYTIC SITUATION

In our discussion of clinical interventions, we distinguished those which reflect psychopathology rooted in developmental arrests from those which reflect psychopathology rooted in intrapsychic conflicts. The analyst's interpretive activity must be attuned to the nuances of self-object differentiation, representational integration, and to their failures. Let us now examine the therapeutic context in which these interpretations are embedded.

The psychoanalytic situation has been examined along three dimensions—the transference, the therapeutic alliance, and the "real" relationship (Stone, 1961; Greenson, 1967). Having developed our understanding of a variety of clinical phenomena from the standpoint of self and object representations, their varying degrees of structuralization, and their defensive and conflictual involvements, we will now re-examine these three dimensions of the treatment situation in the light of this new understanding.

The Transference

Though transference is a universal phenomenon, the concept has a history and usage specific to the analytic situation. Implicit in the concept of transference is the assumption of the analyst's neutrality. The analyst refrains from introducing his own archaic representational configurations into the treatment and from amalgamating, recasting, or warding off the patient's images of himself, the therapist, and their relationship. Instead, the analyst aims to unveil and illuminate the patient's representational world so that developmentally arrested configurations may be articulated and warded-off representations may be reassimilated.

The analyst's neutrality enables both patient and therapist to observe the defensive revival, wishful reproduction, and anxiety-arousing repetition of past object relations and conflicts. Such replicative revivals indicate that certain developmental prerequisites have been met.

They indicate that self and object representations have been differentiated, integrated, and consolidated. Mental contents can then be transposed from one representation to another. The original representations which were the source of the content are unencumbered, as the transference object becomes the new target of the displaced affects and wishes.

By virtue of the analyst's neutrality, the revived conflictual representational configurations can be observed in the analytic situation in a clear and intensified form. Past unresolved conflicts are repeated with the analyst. An array of defensive activities springing from past conflicts as well as from their current revival in the therapeutic interaction is brought into play. Thus, certain nuclear representational configurations are reanimated, experienced in relation to the analyst, and better understood. Interpretations by the analyst enable the patient to reassimilate what he has needed to ward off. This description applies to classical transference analysis. In our work it has been exemplified by the analyses of Anna, Reginald, Rachel, and Joan.

Viewed from this vantage point, the question of whether transference entails only displacements from past object relationships or also encompasses projections of id, ego, and superego functions is moot. Once self-object boundaries have been consolidated, the revival of past representational configurations can evoke any defensive activity, including the defensive translocation of contents across those boundaries, as in projection, or the defensive dissolution of those boundaries.

With patients whose pathology has been conceptualized in terms of developmental arrests, whereby self and object representations have remained incompletely differentiated and integrated, we cannot assume that the analyst will be experienced as a separate and whole person. For these patients, for whom Kohut (1971) used the term "transferencelike phenomena" and to whom Kernberg (1975) attributes "narcissistic resistance," the analyst remains an archaic selfobject.

Just as we proposed a developmental line for defensive processes, whereby we could distinguish a defense proper from its prestages, we are now proposing a distinction between the precursors or *prestages of transference* and its classical form.

When the analyst serves as a selfobject, the patient does not displace into the analytic relationship a representational structure which was consolidated in his past, but rather is continuing to experience his developmentally determined inability to maintain differentiated and integrated self and object representations, as well as his need for an archaic tie to substitute for precarious or missing psychic structure. Corresponding to a predominance in the analytic situation of these developmental incapacities and archaic needs (prestages of transference), prestages of various defenses will tend to pervade the analytic material. Our clinical cases exemplified this with respect to the prestages of defensive idealization, projection, incorporation, and splitting.

The analytic interventions discussed in the previous section are aimed at promoting the differentiation and integration of arrested representational configurations. Where once the analyst was experienced predominantly as an archaic selfobject, he will gradually become a separate and whole object and, hence, a target of more classical neurotic transference. "Where the selfobject was, there the constant transference object shall be."

The Therapeutic Alliance

A prerequisite for the establishment and maintenance

of a therapeutic alliance is that self and object representations have in large part become differentiated and integrated. Not until the analyst is recognized and accepted
as a more or less separate and whole object can a reciprocally collaborative relationship be formed. To the extent that self and object representations are vulnerable
and the analyst is needed as a selfobject for the maintenance of the patient's self-cohesion and self-continuity,
a therapeutic alliance will be unavailable in the therapeutic situation. In such cases, the inability to form a
therapeutic alliance is rooted in the same developmental
interferences that produced the patient's psychopathology. Hence, the treatment of structural deficiencies and
developmental arrests and the establishment of a therapeutic alliance are identical processes. The successful
treatment of developmental arrests consolidates the
structural prerequisites for a therapeutic alliance (as in
the case of Mark).

In the treatment of developmental arrests, and thus
in the establishment of a therapeutic alliance, the analyst's empathy plays a crucial role, compensating for developmental voids in the patient. The patient's experience
of the analyst's empathic communications may be viewed
as a precursor or *prestage of a therapeutic alliance*. Joint
explorations of various aspects of the patient's life and
difficulties may at times be undertaken, but the patient
will tend to experience the analyst's empathic understanding as a revival of early mergers, whereby the analyst becomes established as an archaic selfobject. Thus,
the prestages of transference and prestages of a therapeutic alliance will coincide and will be indistinguishable
from one another as primitive states pervade the analytic
situation.

Empathic communication is to be distinguished from
a therapeutic "misalliance" (Langs, 1975) in that in the

former the analyst's understanding of the patient's representational world does not constitute an agreement with the patient as to its actuality but rather a comprehension of its psychological meaning and impact. Empathic communications are those which elucidate aspects of the patient's representational world, including its affective nuances. The analyst speaks, thereby, not as an outside observer describing a manifest interpersonal event but from the vantage point of the patient's psychic reality. Furthermore, when treating developmental arrests, he accepts the psychic reality of the patient that he, the analyst, must serve as a selfobject. He does not demand of the patient that he be accepted as a separate and whole object, although as this developmental milestone is achieved, he will recognize and acknowledge it. By accepting his role as a selfobject, the analyst is in a position to make a contribution to the patient's capacity for self-observation through the eventual internalization of the empathic bond which becomes established.

The analyst's acceptance of the role of selfobject has several consequences for the conduct and course of treatment. Most important, he does not interfere with the unfolding of the patient's arrested representational configurations (Kohut, 1971). He therefore avoids a repetition of the traumatic interferences with self-object differentiation and representational integration that come about through prematurely ruptured selfobject ties or phase-inappropriate depletions of idealized images of the self or parental objects. Consequently, he is more likely to be regarded with trust and admitted, gradually, into the more vulnerable, shame-ridden areas of the patient's past and present life.

The analyst's empathic communications will include clarifications of the content, affective nuances, and functions of the selfobject configurations that the patient attempts to revive or maintain in the face of threats of regressive fragmentation or dissolution. Indications that steps toward greater differentiation and integration have been taken are acknowledged as well. Further advances in differentiation and integration are then made possible by the increased confidence the patient feels in the consolidation of earlier steps. We assume a continuous fluctuation between attempts to maintain an achieved but as yet precariously consolidated position and progressive strivings for still greater differentiation and integration of self and object images. The analyst's accurate grasp of these fluctuating nuances constitutes the correct, requisite empathic understanding. It enables the patient to maintain and consolidate what has been attained and concurrently to reach toward what is yet to be achieved.

Through his careful attention to the patient's subjective world, the analyst gradually enables the patient to structure that world with differentiated and integrated self and object representations. In this way a therapeutic alliance becomes a possibility in the analytic situation. We have shown that the analyst must be alert to signals from the patient that he is no longer needed as a selfobject, but can be experienced as a "new," more or less separate and whole object. Only when the analyst is established as this "new" object can a therapeutic alliance be formed, wherein an analysis of warded-off conflicts can be undertaken without producing devastating narcissistic injuries or dangerous structural decompensations.

Once a therapeutic alliance is established, the possibility of reversals to prestages in which self and object images are merged and unintegrated remains ever present. This may occur either as a defensive regression or as a disintegration of newly acquired representational structure which is as yet insufficiently consolidated. The analyst must be attuned to these shifts, which may occur in consequence of minute failures of empathic understanding on his part or, in cases of defensive regression, in reaction to the arousal of intrapsychic conflicts. Analytic exploration of the precipitating events must not be complicated by the analyst's failure to recognize or acknowledge lapses in empathic understanding.

The occurrence of prestages of transference thus coincides with the necessity of establishing a therapeutic alliance. Once established, the existence of a therapeutic alliance makes possible classical transference interpretations in the context of structural conflict. At times, the transference may obliterate an operative therapeutic alliance—for example, when the transference becomes excessively hostile or eroticized. The analyst may then either attempt to revitalize the "absent" alliance or offer direct interpretations of the transference. These temporary obliterations of the therapeutic alliance, which can occur even in the treatment of classical transference neuroses, must be distinguished from instances in which the vulnerable structuralizations and precarious therapeutic alliance achieved in the treatment of developmental arrests regressively dissolve into their archaic prestages.

The "Real" Relationship

The "real" relationship between patient and therapist was introduced as a dimension of the therapeutic situation because, presumably, neither the transference nor the therapeutic alliance enabled analysts to include their human qualities within a conceptualization of analytic treatment. Indeed, in discussions of severe psychopathology, treatment success is sometimes attributed to the analyst's "human" concern, dedication, and, especially his warmth. There are certain dangers inherent in this idea, however. To view the real relationship as a non-transference and nonanalyzable dimension of the treatment situation opens the door for the introduction of parameters without analytic safeguards. Furthermore, while transference phenomena can be documented through the associative unfolding of the patient's life history and the operation of a therapeutic alliance can be inferred from the quality of the treatment sessions, the real relationship refers to a dimension of the therapeutic situation which remains solely within the realm of the analyst's impressions. So long as the analyst remains predominantly a selfobject, what may be a real relationship for the analyst could be an archaic merger for the patient.

Appreciation, admiration, and respect for the analyst as analyst, as well as recognition of his shortcomings and limitations, indicate a delineation of the analyst as a separate and whole object. For structurally deficient patients, such perceptions of the analyst as a "real" object become possible only when there has been sufficient working through of the arrested developmental aspects of the patient's pathology so that the analyst is no longer required to serve as an archaic selfobject and the revival of intrapsychic conflicts has begun to predominate in the therapeutic relationship. The analyst should, of course, behave in a human and humane way with all his patients, but there is no reason why the patient's varying perceptions of these attributes and his reactions to them should be beyond analysis.

Through the distinction between the transference and the real relationship, analysts have attempted to avoid a particular pitfall. For the analyst to imply that all the patient's perceptions of and reactions to him are "distortions" transferred from the past may communicate to the patient that nothing he sees or feels is real. However, an approach which seeks to understand and illuminate the representational configurations into which a particular impression is assimilated both avoids the danger of undermining the patient's sense of reality and promotes the continuing articulation of self and object images.

The establishment of the analyst as a "realistically" perceived object is one of the developmental prerequisites for a therapeutic alliance. The perception of the analyst as an increasingly differentiated, empathically inquiring object enables the patient to evolve a complimentary representation of himself as a person who has been and can be empathically understood and who can eventually, through internalization, empathically understand himself. The establishment of these representational structures serves as a nucleus to which others may be amalgamated (e.g., transference configurations) and from which others may be discriminated as treatment progresses. The "real" relationship is thus not only what remains after the transference has been analyzed, it is also what has been acquired and consolidated through the structuralizations of the patient's representational world which have enabled him to form a reciprocally collaborative bond with the analyst.

In the treatment of structurally deficient patients, all three components of the classical analytic situation—the "real" relationship, the therapeutic alliance, and the transference proper—gradually evolve from their archaic prestages as structuralization proceeds. Hence, the eventual differentiation and crystallization of these three components of the analytic situation may be viewed as a developmental achievement which constitutes a central therapeutic goal in the treatment of developmental arrests.

THE THERAPEUTIC AND UNTHERAPEUTIC ACTION OF PSYCHOANALYSIS

In the treatment of classical conflict pathology, the desired outcome of analysis and therefore of mutative interpretations is typically referred to as "structural change." Such change has been conceptualized metapsychologically in terms of structural realignments whereby conscious and volitional ego functioning increasingly supplants unconscious id and superego functions. How is this process to be understood in terms of the patient's world of self and object representations? In consequence of the therapeutic regression, early conflictual self and object images, together with the sexual, aggressive, defensive, and other relations linking them, are displaced from the patient's unconscious infantile history into the analytic relationship. In the working-through phase, the repeated interpretation of the nature, genetic origins, and multiple functions of these transference configurations gradually frees the patient's mental life from the grip of unconscious conflict. This therapeutic action of psychoanalysis has been explained in terms of the patient's rational renunciation of infantile wishes liberated through the analysis of transference resistances (Freud, 1912, 1913, 1914b, 1915b, 1937; A. Freud, 1936), the introjection of the analyst into the patient's superego functioning (Strachey, 1934), the patient's discovery of new modes of object relationship with the analyst (Loewald, 1960), or the reorganization and transformation of the patient's subjective world from one which is restricted by past self and object representations to one which encompasses the realities and richer variety of past and current self and object experiences (Schafer, 1968; Stolorow et al., 1978).

All such formulations of structural change and ther-

apeutic action have in common the assumption that the
patient has achieved certain pivotal developmental milestones. The concept of realigning id, ego, and superego
functions presupposes that a certain minimum degree of
consolidation of those functions has occurred. Similarly,
the concept of reorganizing and transforming infantile
self and object representations which have been displaced
into the analytic relationship presupposes that a minimum degree of articulation, differentiation, and integration of those representations has been accomplished.
Furthermore, it implies that the patient has acquired at
least a rudimentary capacity to distinguish the displaced
imagery from images of a "real" relationship and therapeutic alliance with the analyst.

Self and object representations that have not yet been
structuralized can be neither displaced nor restructured.
Hence, formulations of structural change appropriate for
cases of classical conflict pathology will not provide a
suitable framework to guide the treatment of structurally
deficient, developmentally arrested patients. With these
latter patients, in whom self and object representations
have remained insufficiently consolidated and vulnerable to regressive decompensation, a different conceptualization of the therapeutic action of psychoanalysis is
required. In such cases, analytic treatment strives not so
much for the realignment of existing pathological structures, but rather for the maturation of representational
structure that is missing or deficient as a consequence
of developmental interferences (Kohut, 1971).

With developmentally arrested patients, therapeutic
action can be found in those psychoanalytic procedures
which facilitate the structuralization of their representational worlds, most notably by promoting the gradual
differentiation and integration of self and object representations within the therapeutic relationship. As a pre-

requisite for such therapeutic action, the patient must be permitted to revive in relation to the analyst those archaic phases at which his representational development had been arrested, and thereby to revitalize those developmental thrusts which had been traumatically or phase-inappropriately aborted. For prolonged periods, the analyst's primary interpretive activity will focus empathically on the primitive, arrested representational configurations that the patient needs to restore or maintain, as, for example, when the patient requires a sense of continuous union with the analyst as an archaic mirroring or idealized selfobject in order to sustain a sense of self-cohesion and to prevent feelings of self-fragmentation. The analyst will also acknowledge the patient's arrival at developmental milestones, as when the resumption of a prematurely interrupted merger gives way to genuine strides toward intrapsychic separation.

The analyst's neutrality and consistent understanding of the patient's archaic states and needs not only contribute to the articulation of the patient's representational world but also function as a "holding environment" (Winnicott, 1965; Modell, 1976). The therapeutic action of this environment is to provide a facilitating medium reinstating the developmental processes of representational differentiation and integration that had been traumatically aborted and arrested during the patient's formative years. As Kohut (1971) has shown, further structuralization is promoted by the repeated analysis of the patient's reactions to nontraumatic empathic failures and other manageable disappointments by the archaically experienced analyst. Such working through fosters the gradual internalization of a differentiated image of the analyst as an understanding presence and, eventually, the development of an autonomous capacity for empathic self-observation, a crucial milestone which makes possible the patient's entry into a therapeutic alliance.

We are now in a position to understand those unfortunate occurrences in the treatment of developmentally arrested patients when the action of psychoanalysis in general, and "correct" interpretations in particular, has proven to be singularly untherapeutic—indeed, countertherapeutic. With increasing knowledge of the psychology of developmental arrests, it is no longer satisfactory to explain such "negative therapeutic reactions" exclusively in terms of the patient's unconscious sense of guilt, need for punishment, and primary masochism (Freud, 1923, 1937), his narcissistic character resistances (Abraham, 1919), his need to ward off the depressive position through omnipotent control (Riviere, 1936), or his unconscious envy of the analyst and resulting complusion to spoil the analytic work (Klein, 1957; Kernberg, 1975).

We suggest that many therapeutic impasses and disasters are the product of a specific failure in empathy, wherein the analyst misunderstands and misinterprets the meaning of the patient's archaic states by amalgamating them to his own much more differentiated and integrated world of self and object representations. Such misunderstandings typically take the form of erroneously interpreting remnants of developmental arrests as if they were expressions of resistances defending against intrapsychic conflicts. When the patient revives an arrested archaic state or need, or attempts a previously aborted developmental step within the analytic relationship, and the analyst interprets this developmental necessity as if it were merely a pathological resistance, the patient will experience such a misinterpretation as a gross failure of empathy, a severe breach of trust. In short, a traumatic narcissistic injury will be inflicted similar in its impact to those in the patient's life which originally produced the developmental arrest (Balint, 1969; Kohut, 1971, 1977). Is it surprising that such misunderstandings can bring negative—often dramatically negative—"therapeutic" reactions in their wake?

In his approach to the treatment of borderline and narcissistic disorders, Kernberg (1975) emphasizes the systematic interpretation of the patient's transference resistances, which he views as primitive defenses against conflictual pregenital aggression. We are suggesting that such an approach is appropriate only for those patients who have achieved the prerequisite degree of differentiation and integration of self and object representations. Kernberg also describes the paranoid transference psychoses, suicidal depressions, and destructive and self-destructive acting out which occur in the course of his treating such patients. We suggest that with any such untoward reaction to the analytic process the analyst must ask: Is this the inevitable result of correctly analyzing primitive defenses against aggression? Or is this the result of a failure to recognize the arrested developmental aspects of the patient's psychopathology so that vital developmental requirements revived in relation to the analyst have once again met with traumatically unempathic responses? In the treatment of developmentally arrested patients, the answers which the analyst finds to such questions will be crucial in determining whether the action of the analysis will eventually prove therapeutic or countertherapeutic.

References

Abraham, K. (1919), A particular form of neurotic resistance against the psycho-analytic method. In: *Selected Papers on Psychoanalysis*. New York: Basic Books, 1960, pp. 303-311.

Apfelbaum, B. (1965), Ego psychology, psychic energy, and the hazards of quantative explanation in psychoanalytic theory. *Internat. J. Psycho-Anal.*, 46:168-182.

Arlow, J. (1963), Conflict, regression, and symptom formation. *Internat. J. Psycho-Anal.*, 44:12-22.

―――― (1966), Depersonalization and derealization. In: *Psychoanalysis—A General Psychology: Essays in Honor of Heinz Hartmann*, ed. R. Loewenstein et al. New York: International Universities Press, pp. 456-478.

―――― & Brenner, C. (1964), *Psychoanalytic Concepts and the Structural Theory*. New York: International Universities Press.

Atkin, S. (1975), Ego synthesis and cognition in a borderline case. *Psychanal. Quart.*, 44:29-61.

Atwood, G. (1977), A patient's claim to paranormal powers. *Amer. J. Psychoanal.*, 37:85-88.

Bach, S. (1975), Narcissism, continuity and the uncanny. *Internat. J. Psycho-Anal.*, 56:77-86.

―――― (1977), On the narcissistic state of consciousness. *Internat. J. Psycho-Anal.*, 58:209-233.

―――― & Schwartz, L. (1972), A dream of the Marquis de Sade: psychoanalytic reflections on narcissistic trauma, decompensation, and the reconsititution of a delusional self. *J. Amer. Psychoanal. Assn.*, 20:451-475.

Bak, R. (1946), Masochism in paranoia. *Psychoanal. Quart.*, 15:285-301.

Balint, M. (1960), Primary narcissism and primary love. *Psychoanal. Quart.*, 29:6-43.

193

———— (1969), Trauma and object relations. *Internat. J. Psycho-Anal.*, 50:429-435.

Bergler, E. (1949), *The Basic Neurosis, Oral Regression and Psychic Masochism*. New York: Grune & Stratton.

———— & Eidelberg, L. (1935), Der mechanismus der depersonalization. *Internat. Zeitsch. Psychoanal.*, 21:258-286.

Berliner, B. (1947), On some psychodynamics of masochism. *Psychoanal. Quart.*, 16:459-471.

———— (1958), The role of object relations in moral masochism. *Psychoanal. Quart.*, 27:38-56.

Bernstein, I. (1957), The role of narcissism in moral masochism. *Psychoanal. Quart.*, 26:358-377.

Bieber, I. (1966), Sadism and masochism. In: *American Handbook of Psychiatry,* vol. 3, ed. S. Arieti. New York: Basic Books, pp. 318-327.

Blanck, G. & Blanck, R. (1974), *Ego Psychology: Theory and Practice*. New York: Columbia University Press.

Blank, H. (1954), Depression, hypomania, and depersonalization. *Psychoanal. Quart.*, 23:20-37.

Blos, P. (1962), *On Adolescence: A Psychoanalytic Interpretation*. New York: Free Press.

Brenman, M. (1952), On teasing and being teased: And the problem of 'moral masochism.' *The Psychoanalytic Study of the Child,* 7:264-285. New York: International Universities Press.

Brenner, C. (1959), The masochistic character: Genesis and treatment. *J. Amer. Psychoanal. Assn.*, 7:197-226.

Bromberg, W. & Schilder, P. (1933), Death and dying. *Psychoanal. Rev.,* 20:133-135.

———— ———— (1936), The attitude of psychoneurotics toward death. *Psychoanal. Rev.,* 23:1-25.

Brunswick, R. M. (1928), A supplement to Freud's *History of an Infantile Neurosis. Internat. J. Psycho-Anal.,* 9:439-476.

Burgner, M. & Edgcumbe, R. (1972), Some problems in the conceptualization of early object relationships. Part II: The concept of object constancy. *The Psychoanalytic Study of the Child,* 27:315-333. New York: Quadrangle.

Bychowski, G. (1959), Some aspects of masochistic involvement. *J. Amer. Psychoanal. Assn.*, 7:248-273.

Caldwell, R. (1976), Primal identity. *Internat. Rev. Psycho-Anal.,* 3:417-434.

Dahl, H., reporter (1968), Panel on Psychoanalytic Theory of the Instinctual Drives in Relation to Recent Developments. *J. Amer. Psychoanal. Assn.*, 16:613-637.

Deutsch, H. (1930a), Hysterical fate neurosis. In: *Neurosis and Character Types*. New York: International Universities Press, 1965, pp. 14-28.

——— (1930b), The significance of masochism in the mental life of women. In: *The Psychoanalytic Reader*, ed. R. Fliess. New York: International Universities Press, 1948, pp. 195-207.

——— (1942), Some forms of emotional disturbance and their relationship to schizophrenia. In: *Neurosis and Character Types*. New York: International Universities Press, 1965, pp. 262-281.

Dooley, L. (1941), The relation of humor to masochism. *Psychoanal. Rev.*, 28:37-46.

Eidelberg, L. (1959), Humiliation in masochism. *J. Amer. Psychoanal. Assn.*, 7:274-283.

Eisenbud, R.-J. (1967), Masochism revisited. *Psychoanal. Rev.*, 54:561-582.

Eisnitz, A. (1969), Narcissistic object choice, self representation. *Internat. J. Psycho-Anal.*, 50:15-25.

Eissler, K. (1958), Notes on problems of technique in the psychoanalytic treatment of adolescents: With some remarks on perversions. *The Psychoanalytic Study of the Child*, 13:223-254. New York: International Universities Press.

Elkin, H. (1972), On selfhood and the development of ego structures in infancy. *Psychoanal. Rev.*, 59:389-416.

Elkisch, P. (1957), The psychological significance of the mirror. *J. Amer. Psychoanal. Assn.*, 5:235-244.

Erikson, E. (1950), *Childhood and Society*. New York: Norton.

——— (1956), The problem of ego identity. In: *Identity and the Life Cycle (Psychological Issues*, Monogr. 1). New York: International Universities Press, 1959, pp. 101-171.

Fast, I. & Chethik, M. (1976), Aspects of depersonalization-derealization in the experience of children. *Internat. Rev. Psycho-Anal.*, 3:483-490.

Federn, P. (1927), Narcissism in the structure of the ego. In: *Ego Psychology and the Psychoses*. New York: Basic Books, 1952, pp. 38-59.

——— (1952), *Ego Psychology and the Psychoses*. New York: Basic Books.

Fenichel, O. (1925), The clinical aspect of the need for punishment. In: *Collected Papers*, first series. New York: Norton, 1953, pp. 71-92.

——— (1935), A critique of the death instinct. In: *Collected Papers*, first series. New York: Norton, 1953, pp. 363-372.

——— (1945), *The Psychoanalytic Theory of Neurosis*. New York: Norton.

Ferenczi, S. (1913), Stages in the development of the sense of reality. In: *Contributions to Psycho-Analysis*. New York: Basic Books/Brunner, 1950, pp. 213-239.

Fine, B., Joseph, E., & Waldhorn, H., eds. (1969), *The Mechanism of Denial; The Manifest Content of the Dream. Kris Study Group*,

Mongr. 3. New York: International Universities Press.

Fleming, J. (1972), Early object deprivation and transference phenomena: The working alliance. *Psychoanal. Quart.*, 41:23-39.

Fliess, R. (1948), An ontogenetic table. In: *The Psychoanalytic Reader*, ed. R. Fliess. New York: International Universities Press, pp. 285-290.

Frances, A. & Dunn, P. (1975), The attachment-autonomy conflict in agoraphobia. *Internat. J. Psycho-Anal.*, 56:435-439.

――― Sacks, M., & Aronoff, M. (1977), Depersonalization: A self-relations perspective. *Internat. J. Psycho-Anal.*, 58:325-331.

Freeman, T. (1964), Some aspects of pathological narcissism. *J. Amer. Psychoanal. Assn.*, 12:540-561.

Freud, A. (1936), *The Ego and the Mechanisms of Defense. Writings*, 2. New York: International Universities Press, 1966.

――― (1965), *Normality and Pathology in Childhood: Assessments of Development. Writings*, 6. New York: International Universities Press.

Freud, S. (1905a), Fragment of an analysis of a case of hysteria. *Standard Edition*, 7:3-122. London: Hogarth Press, 1953.

――― (1905b), Three essays on the theory of sexuality. *Standard Edition,* 7:125-243. London: Hogarth Press, 1953.

――― (1911a), Formulations on the two principles of mental functioning. *Standard Edition*, 12:215-226. London: Hogarth Press, 1958.

――― (1911b), Psycho-analytic notes on an autobiographical account of a case of paranoia (dementia paranoides). *Standard Edition*, 12:3-82. London: Hogarth Press, 1958.

――― (1912), The dynamics of transference. *Standard Edition*, 12:99-108. London: Hogarth Press, 1958.

――― (1913), On beginning the treatment. *Standard Edition*, 12:122-144. London: Hogarth Press, 1958.

――― (1914a), On narcissism: An introduction. *Standard Edition*, 14:69-102. London: Hogarth Press, 1957.

――― (1914b), Remembering, repeating and working through. *Standard Edition*, 12:146-156. London: Hogarth Press, 1958.

――― (1915a), Instincts and their vicissitudes. *Standard Edition*, 14:111-140. London: Hogarth Press, 1957.

――― (1915b), Observations on transference love. *Standard Edition*, 12:158-171. London: Hogarth Press, 1958.

――― (1916), Some character types met with in psychoanalytic work. *Standard Edition*, 14:310-333. London: Hogarth Press, 1957.

――― (1917), Mourning and melancholia. *Standard Edition*, 14:239-258. London: Hogarth Press, 1957.

――― (1919a), 'A child is being beaten': A contribution to the study of the origin of sexual perversions. *Standard Edition*, 17:177-204. London: Hogarth Press, 1955.

—— (1919b), The "uncanny." *Standard Edition*, 17:218-252. London: Hogarth Press, 1955.

—— (1922), Some neurotic mechanisms in jealousy, paranoia and homosexuality. *Standard Edition*, 18:222-232. London: Hogarth Press, 1955.

—— (1923), The ego and the id. *Standard Edition*, 19:3-66. London: Hogarth Press, 1961.

—— (1924), The economic problem of masochism. *Standard Edition*, 19:157-170. London: Hogarth Press, 1961.

—— (1926), Inhibitions, symptoms and anxiety. *Standard Edition*, 20:77-174. London: Hogarth Press, 1959.

—— (1927), Fetishism. *Standard Edition*, 21:149-157. London: Hogarth Press, 1961.

—— (1928), Dostoevsky and parricide. *Standard Edition*, 21:175-194. London: Hogarth Press, 1961.

—— (1933), New introductory lectures on psycho-analysis. *Standard Edition*, 22:3-182. London: Hogarth Press, 1964.

—— (1936), A disturbance of memory on the Acropolis. *Standard Edition*, 22:238-248. London: Hogarth Press, 1964.

—— (1937), Analysis terminable and interminable. *Standard Edition*, 23:211-253. London: Hogarth Press, 1964.

—— (1940), An outline of psycho-analysis. *Standard Edition*, 23:141-207. London: Hogarth Press, 1964.

Fromm, E. (1973), *The Anatomy of Human Destructiveness*. New York: Holt, Rinehart & Winston.

Gedo, J. & Goldberg, A. (1973), *Models of the Mind*. Chicago: University of Chicago Press.

Gero, G. (1962), Sadism, masochism, and aggression: Their role in symptom-formation. *Psychoanal. Quart.*, 31:32-42.

Glover, E. (1955), *The Technique of Psychoanalysis*. New York: International Universities Press.

Goldberg, A. (1975), A fresh look at perverse behavior. *Internat. J. Psycho-Anal.*, 56:335-342.

Grand, H. (1973), The masochistic defence of the 'double mask.' *Internat. J. Psycho-Anal.*, 54:445-454.

Greenacre, P. (1958), Early physical determinants in the development of the sense of identity. In: *Emotional Growth*. New York: International Universities Press, 1971, pp. 113-127.

Greenson, R. (1967), *The Technique and Practice of Psychoanalysis*. New York: International Universities Press.

Grossman, W. & Stewart, W. (1976), Penis envy: from childhood wish to developmental metaphor. *J. Amer. Psychoanal. Assn.*, 24 (Suppl.):193-212.

Guntrip, H. (1969), *Schizoid Phenomena, Object-Relations, and the Self*. New York: International Universities Press.

Hartmann, H. (1939), *Ego Psychology and the Problem of Adaptation*.

New York: International Universities Press, 1958.

——— (1950), Comments on the psychoanalytic theory of the ego. In: *Essays on Ego Psychology*. New York: International Universities Press, 1964, pp. 113-141.

Hoffer, W. (1950), Development of the body ego. *The Psychoanalytic Study of the Child*, 5:18-23. New York: International Universities Press.

Horney, K. (1935), The problem of feminine masochism. *Psychoanal. Rev.*, 22:241-257.

Jacobson, E. (1959), The "exceptions": An elaboration of Freud's character study. *The Psychoanalytic Study of the Child*, 14:135-154. New York: International Universities Press.

——— (1964), *The Self and the Object World*. New York: International Universities Press.

——— (1971), *Depression*. New York: International Universities Press.

Joffe, W. & Sandler, J. (1967), Some conceptual problems involved in the consideration of disorders of narcissism. *J. Child Psychother.*, 2:56-66.

Joseph, E., ed. (1965), *Beating Fantasies. Kris Study Group*, Monogr. 1. New York: International Universities Press.

Kanzer, M. (1964), Freud's use of the terms "autoerotism" and "narcissism." *J. Amer. Psychoanal. Assn.*, 12:529-539.

Keiser, S. (1949), The fear of sexual passivity in the masochist. *Internat. J. Psycho-Anal.*, 30:162-171.

Kernberg, O. (1975), *Borderline Conditions and Pathological Narcissism*. New York: Jason Aronson.

——— (1976), *Object Relations Theory and Clinical Psychoanalysis*. New York: Jason Aronson.

Klein, G. (1976), Freud's two theories of sexuality. In: *Psychoanalytic Theory: An Exploration of Essentials*. New York: International Universities Press, pp. 72-120.

Klein, M. (1935), A contribution to the psychogenesis of manic-depressive states. In: *Contributions to Psychoanalysis 1921-1945*. London: Hogarth Press, 1948, pp. 282-310.

——— (1957), *Envy and Gratitude*. New York: Basic Books.

Kohut, H. (1971), *The Analysis of the Self*. New York: International Universities Press.

——— (1972), Thoughts on narcissism and narcissistic rage. In: *The Search for the Self*. New York: International Universities Press, 1978, pp. 615-658.

——— (1977), *The Restoration of the Self*. New York: International Universities Press.

Lacan, J. (1949), The mirror stage as formative of the function of the I as revealed in psychoanalytic experience. In: *Ecrits*. New York: Norton, 1977, pp. 1-7.

Lachmann, F. (1975), Homosexuality: Some diagnostic perspectives and dynamic considerations. *Amer. J. Psychother.*, 29:254-260.

Langs, R. (1975), Therapeutic misalliances. *Internat. J. Psychoanal. Psychother.*, 4:77-105.

Levitan, H. (1967), Depersonalization and the dream. *Psychoanal. Quart.*, 36:157-171.

—— (1969), The depersonalizing process. *Psychoanal. Quart.*, 38:97-109.

—— (1970), The depersonalization process. The sense of reality and unreality. *Psychoanal. Quart.*, 39:449-470.

Lewin, B. (1950), *The Psychoanalysis of Elation*. New York: The Psychoanalytic Quarterly.

—— (1954), Sleep, narcissistic neurosis, and the analytic situation. In: *Selected Writings*. New York: The Psychoanalytic Quarterly, Inc., 1973, pp. 227-247.

Lichtenstein, H. (1961), Identity and sexuality: A study of their interrelationship in man. *J. Amer. Psychoanal. Assn.*, 9:179-260.

—— (1964), The role of narcissism in the emergence and maintenance of a primary identity. *Internat. J. Psycho-Anal.*, 45:49-56.

Loewald, H. (1960), On the therapeutic action of psychoanalysis. *Internat. J. Psycho-Anal.*, 41:16-33.

Loewenstein, R. (1945), A special form of self-punishment. *Psychoanal. Quart.*, 14:46-61.

—— (1957), A contribution to the psychoanalytic theory of masochism. *J. Amer. Psychoanal. Assn.*, 5:197-234.

Mahler, M. (1960), Perceptual de-differentiation and psychotic "object relationship." *Internat. J. Psycho-Anal.*, 41:548-553.

—— Pine, F. & Bergman, A. (1975), *The Psychological Birth of the Human Infant*. New York: Basic Books.

Menaker, E. (1953), Masochism—a defense reaction of the ego. *Psychoanal. Quart.*, 22:205-220.

Modell, A. (1976), The "holding environment" and the therapeutic action of psychoanalysis. *J. Amer. Psychoanal. Assn.*, 24:285-307.

Monchy, R. de (1950), Masochism as a pathological and as a normal phenomenon in the human mind. *Internat. J. Psycho-Anal.*, 31:95-97.

Murray, J. (1964), Narcissism and the ego ideal. *J. Amer. Psychoanal. Assn.*, 12:477-511.

M'Uzan, M. de (1973), A case of masochistic perversion and outline of a theory. *Internat. J. Psycho-Anal.*, 54:455-467.

Nagy, M. (1959), The child's view of death. In: *The Meaning of Death*, ed. H. Feifel. New York: McGraw-Hill, pp. 79-98.

Neubauer, P. (1960), The one-parent child and his Oedipal development. *The Psychoanalytic Study of the Child*, 15:286-309. New

York: International Universities Press.

Niederland, W. (1951), Three notes on the Schreber case. *Psycho-anal. Quart.*, 20:579-591.

Nunberg, H. (1924), States of depersonalization in the light of the libido theory. In: *Practice and Theory of Psychoanalysis.* New York: International Universities Press, 1961, pp. 60-74.

—— (1926), The sense of guilt and the need for punishment. In: *Practice and Theory of Psychoanalysis.* New York: International Universities Press, 1961, pp. 89-101.

—— (1932), *Principles of Psychoanalysis: Their Application to the Neuroses.* New York: International Universities Press, 1955.

Nydes, J. (1950), The magical experience of the masturbation fantasy. *Amer. J. Psychother.*, 4:303-310.

—— (1963), Schreber, parricide, and paranoid-masochism. *Internat. J. Psycho-Anal.*, 44:208-212.

Oberndorf, C. (1950, The role of anxiety in depersonalization. *Internat. J. Psycho-Anal.*, 31:1-5.

Oremland, J. & Windholz, E. (1971), Some specific transference, coun-tertransference and supervisory problems in the analysis of a narcissistic personality. *Internat. J. Psycho-Anal.*, 52:267-275.

Ostow, M., ed. (1974), *Sexual Deviation/Psychoanalytic Insights.* New York: Quadrangle/New York Times Book Co.

Panken, S. (1973), *The Joy of Suffering.* New York: Jason Aronson.

Paul, M. & Carson, I. (1976), The sense of strangeness. *Internat. Rev. Psycho-Anal.*, 3:435-440.

Pruyser, P. (1975), What splits in "splitting"? A scrutiny of the concept of splitting in psychoanalysis and psychiatry. *Bull. Menninger Clinic*, 39:1-46.

Pulver, S. (1970), Narcissism: The term and the concept. *J. Amer. Psychoanal. Assn.*, 18:319-341.

Rank, O. (1929), *Will Therapy and Truth and Reality.* New York: Knopf, 1972.

Rapaport, D. (1951), The conceptual model of psychoanalysis. *J. Per-sonality*, 20:56-81.

Reich, A. (1953), Narcissistic object choice in women. In: *Psychoan-alytic Contributions.* New York: International Universities Press, 1973, pp. 179-202.

—— (1960), Pathological forms of self-esteem regulation. In: *Psy-choanalytic Contributions.* New York: International Universi-ties Press, 1973, pp. 288-311.

Reich, W. (1933-1934), *Character Analysis.* New York: Touchstone Books, 1974.

Reik, T. (1941), *Masochism in Modern Man.* New York: Farrar & Strauss.

Riviere, J. (1936), A contribution to the analysis of the negative ther-apeutic reaction. *Internat. J. Psycho-Anal.*, 17:304-320.

Rochlin, G. (1973), *Man's Aggression: The Defense of the Self.* Boston: Gambit.

Rosenfeld, H. (1947), Analysis of a schizophrenic state with depersonalization. In: *Psychotic States.* New York: International Universities Press, 1966, pp. 13-33.

——— (1964a), The psychopathology of hypochondriasis. In: *Psychotic States.* New York: International Universities Press, 1966, pp. 180-199.

——— (1964b), On the psychopathology of narcissism: A clinical approach. In: *Psychotic States.* New York: International Universities Press, 1966, pp. 169-179.

Ross, J. (1977), Towards fatherhood: The epigenesis of paternal identity during a boy's first decade. *Internat. Rev. Psycho-Anal.,* 4:327-348.

Ross, N. (1970), The primacy of genitality in the light of ego psychology: Introductory remarks. *J. Amer. Psychoanal. Assn.,* 18:267-284.

Sandler, J. & Rosenblatt, B. (1962), The concept of the representational world. *The Psychoanalytic Study of the Child,* 17:128-145. New York: International Universities Press.

Sarlin, C. (1962), Depersonalization and derealization. *J. Amer. Psychoanal. Assn.,* 10:784-804.

Schafer, R. (1967), Ideals, the ego ideal, and the ideal self. In: *Motives and Thoughts. Psychoanalytic Essays in Honor of David Rapaport,* ed. R. Holt. (*Psychological Issues,* Monogr. 18/19). New York: International Universities Press, pp. 131-174.

——— (1968), *Aspects of Internalization.* New York: International Universities Press.

Searles, H. (1959), Integration and differentiation in schizophrenia: An over-all view. *Brit. J. Med. Psychol.,* 32:261-281.

Socarides, C. (1958), The function of moral masochism: With special reference to the defence processes. *Internat. J. Psycho-Anal.,* 39:587-597.

——— (1969), Psychoanalytic therapy of a male homosexual. *Psychoanal. Quart.,* 38:173-190.

——— (1973), Sexual perversion and the fear of engulfment. *Internat. J. Psychoanal. Psychother.,* 2:432-448.

——— (1974), The demonified mother: A study of voyeurism and sexual sadism. *Internat. Rev. Psycho-Anal., 1:187-195.*

——— (1978), *Homosexuality,* New York: Jason Aronson.

——— (1979), A unitary theory of sexual perversion. In: *On Sexuality: Psychoanalytic Observations,* ed. T.B. Karasu & C. W. Socarides. New York: International Universities Press, pp. 161-188.

Spitz, R. (1959), *A Genetic Field Theory of Ego Formation.* New York: International Universities Press.

—— (1961), Some early prototypes of ego defenses. *J. Amer. Psychoanal. Assn.,* 9:626-651.

—— (1963), Life and the dialogue. In: *Counterpoint: Libidinal Object and Subject,* ed. H. Gaskill. *New York: International Universities Press, pp. 154-176.*

—— (1964), The derailment of dialogue. *J. Amer. Psychoanal. Assn.,* 12:752-775.

—— (1965), *The First Year of Life.* New York: International Universities Press.

—— (1966), Metapsychology and direct infant observation. In: *Psychoanalysis—a General Psychology: Essays in Honor of Heinz Hartmann,* ed. R. Loewenstein, L. Newman, M. Schur and A. Solnit. New York: International Universtities Press, pp. 123-151.

Spruiell, V. (1974), Theories of the treatment of narcissistic personalities. *J. Amer. Psychoanal. Assn.,* 22:268-278.

Stamm, J. (1962), Altered ego states allied to depersonalization. *J. Amer. Psychoanal. Assn.,* 10:762-783.

Stein, M., reporter (1956), Panel on The Problem of Masochism in the Theory and Technique of Psychoanalysis. *J. Amer. Psychoanal. Assn.,* 4:526-538.

Stoller, R. (1975), *Perversion: The Erotic Form of Hatred.* New York: Pantheon Books.

Stolorow, R. (1973), Perspectives on death anxiety: A review. *Psychiat. Quart.,* 47:473-486.

—— & Atwood, G. (1976), An ego-psychological analysis of the work and life of Otto Rank in the light of modern conceptions of narcissism. In: *Faces in a Cloud: Subjectivity in Personality Theory.* New York: Jason Aronson, 1979, pp. 131-171.

—— —— (1979), *Faces in a Cloud: Subjectivity in Personality Theory.* New York: Jason Aronson.

—— —— & Ross, J. (1978), The representational world in psychoanalytic therapy. *Internat. Rev. Psycho-Anal.,* 5:247-256.

Stone, L. (1961), *The Psychoanalytic Situation.* New York: International Universities Press.

Strachey, J. (1934), The nature of the therapeutic action of psychoanalysis. *Internat. J. Psycho-Anal.,* 15:127-159. Reprinted (1969) 50:275-292.

Tausk, V. (1919), On the origin of the "influencing machine" in schizophrenia. *Psychoanal. Quart.,* 2:1933, 519-552.

Tolpin, M. (1971), On the beginnings of a cohesive self: An application of the concept of transmuting internalization to the study of the transitional object and signal anxiety. *The Psychoanalytic Study of the Child,* 26:316-354. New York: Quadrangle Books.

Waelder, R. (1936), The principle of multiple function: Observations on over-determination. In: *Psychoanalysis: Observation, Theory,*

Application, ed. S. A. Guttman. New York: International Universities Press, 1976, pp. 68-83.

———— (1951), The structure of paranoid ideas: A critical survey of various theories. In: *Psychoanalysis: Observation, Theory, Application,* ed. S. A. Guttman. New York: International Universities Press, 1976, pp. 207-228.

Winnicott, D. W. (1945), Primitive emotional development. In: *Through Paediatrics to Psycho-Analysis.* New York: Basic Books, 1975, pp. 145-156.

———— (1960), Ego distortion in terms of true and false self. In: *The Maturational Processes and the Facilitating Environment.* New York: International Universities Press, 1965, pp. 140-152.

———— (1962), Ego integration in child development. In: *The Maturational Processes and the Facilitating Environment.* New York: International Universities Press, 1965, pp. 56-63.

———— (1965), *The Maturational Processes and the Facilitating Environment.* New York: International Universities Press.

———— (1967), Mirror-role of mother and family in child development. In: *Playing and Reality.* New York: Basic Books, 1971, pp. 111-118.

Wolfenstein, M. (1966), How is mourning possible? *The Psychoanalytic Study of the Child,* 21:93-123. New York: International Universities Press.

Zetzel, E. (1966), An obsessional neurotic: Freud's Rat Man. In: *The Capacity for Emotional Growth.* New York: International Universities Press, 1970, pp. 216-228.

INDEX

Abraham, K., 2, 90, 190, 193
Acting out
  analytic approach to, 167-168
  sexual fantasy vs., 144-168
Aggression, 82-85
  analytic approach to, 165-167
  narcissism and vulnerability to,
    40-41
Agoraphobia, 132-133
Anal mode, 147
Anna, 50-62, 102-104, 175, 179
Anxiety, 30, 121-123; see also
    Castration anxiety;
    Conflict, structural; Death
    anxiety; Hypochondriasis
    and hypochondriacal anxiety
Apfelbaum, B., 9, 193
Arieti, S., 194
Arlow, J., 10, 11, 13, 88,
    129-130, 134, 141-142, 193
Aronoff, M., 196
Arrest, developmental, 96-97
  death anxiety and, 125, 141;
    clinical case, 126-128
  definition of, 5
  depersonalization and,
    136-138; clinical cases,
    132-134, 135-136, 138-141
  hypochondriacal aspects of,
    122-125, 141
  idealizations and grandiosity

based on, 64, 85-87;
  clinical cases, 65-74, 81-84
  see also Defenses, prestages
    of; Development
Atkin, S., 95-97, 193; case of,
    107-109, 110, 175
Atwood, G., 1, 3, 126, 135, 193
Audience, 34

Bach, S., 30, 32, 37, 38, 40, 131,
    137-138, 193
Bak, R., 28-30, 32, 193
Balint, M., 18, 112, 190-191,
    193-194
Bergler, E., 29-31, 34, 129, 194
Bergman, A., 199
Berliner, 29, 30, 33-35, 41, 194
Bernstein, I., 30, 31, 36, 38, 194
Bieber, I., 29, 194
Bill, 100-103, 126-128, 137, 139,
    175, 176
Blanck, G., 2, 194
Blanck, R., 2, 194
Blank, H., 129-131, 194
Blos, P., 123, 194
Body image, 145-146
Borderline disorder, 2-3, 22-23,
    32, 36, 93-94, 96, 98,
    107, 108-109
Brenman, M., 29, 34, 39, 149,
    194